To Parents and Educators

Trash! evolved from a series of workshops we conducted with ragpicker children. We decided to write this book on the complex issues of child labour and the environment because we believe that problematic themes have a place in children's literature. Books can deal openly and honestly with the harsher realities of life, which children see around them everyday.

The child's mind between the ages of nine and thirteen expands laterally. It becomes capable of taking in a variety of things—both information as well as emotion. The real world becomes interesting, raising a lot of troubling questions and doubts. We feel these questions must be addressed, because children can and do comprehend the contradictions of the world we live in.

At the same time, most children are natural optimists, so difficult themes need to be dealt with gently and sensitively. A child reader cannot be made directly guilty or responsible for a situation she has not created, and in which she is relatively powerless. Yet she needs to understand that street and working children are like herself, with the same needs and rights. Similarly, she cannot stop the course of environmental degradation, but can think about and take action which is within her control.

Trash! therefore works in two ways:

- to create an empathy and an understanding for working children in the reader, we have worked their real-life experiences into a story. It allows the reader to enter their world in a way which facts alone cannot accomplish.
- the child reader also needs a context in which to place the themes the story raises. So alongside the narrative, we present facts and arguments which do this. They are of two kinds—the first deals with issues connected to child labour, while the second is concerned with environmental questions: garbage disposal, recycling, and papermaking. We also suggest simple ways in which the child can actively deal with these problems.

We end with a discussion on questions the book is likely to raise in the child reader, in which we emphasize that there are no simple solutions to complex and troubling social questions. Yet we need to work through them to reach an understanding which will inform our actions.

Trash!

On Ragpicker Children and Recycling

Gita Wolf

Anushka Ravishankar

Orijit Sen

Tara Publishing

Trash! On Ragpicker Children and Recycling

Editors: V. Geetha, Sirish Rao

Design: Rathna Ramanathan

Production: C. Arumugam

Tara Publishing

38 G/A Shoreham

5th Avenue, Besant Nagar

Chennai 600 090, India

email: tara@vsnl.com

www.tarabooks.com

Printed at The Ind-com Press, Chennai

ISBN 81-86211-69-1

chapter one

Runaway

When the Kanyakumari Express pulled in at Chennai Central, it took Velu some time to get off. When he finally squeezed out and stood on the platform, his legs felt wobbly, as if he was still on a moving train.

"Oy, out of the way!" A porter went by with a loaded trolley. Velu jumped aside.

He sat on a bench on the platform, putting his small bundle down. In all his eleven years, he had never seen so many people, except once a year at the fair in his village. People walked by, bumping into him with their suitcases. A voice announced something on a loudspeaker. Near him a group of people sat on their luggage, looking at a TV hanging from the roof. The noise was terrible.

Velu put his head down on his knees, feeling miserable and exhausted. He had run away from his village two days ago. For two days he had eaten nothing but some peanuts and a piece of jaggery. In his bundle he carried a shirt, a towel and a comb.

He had walked for most of the first day to Karur and then got on the train to Chennai. Velu had no money for a ticket but luckily the ticket collector didn't come to the unreserved compartment. He had tried to sleep on the floor near the door. A group of men next to him had played cards and shouted all night.

"Aiy! What, new to town eh?" called out a rough voice.

Velu opened his eyes. There were a lot of people standing around, but nobody was looking at him.

"Here! Aiy!"

He turned around. Behind him was a girl around his own age, wearing a long banian that came down to her knees. Her hair was stiff and brownish and she had a huge sack on one shoulder. She was picking up dirty plastic cups from the floor and stuffing them into her sack. Why is she calling me, thought Velu. And why is a girl wearing a banian?

"No need to stare stupidly. What's your name?"

"Velu," muttered Velu, looking away.

"So Mr. Velu," said the girl, looking at his bundle. "Run away from home?"

Velu didn't answer. He didn't want to tell some strange girl what he had done. He had run away because he couldn't stand his father beating him for one more day. His father snatched away all the money Velu and his sisters earned and spent it on drink.

"Don't think I don't know. This place is full of children like you. So what are you going to do here? Become rich?"

She sat down next to him. Velu shifted away slightly.

He felt hunger pinching him and pressed his stomach with a grimace.

"Hungry?" asked the girl. "You won't get food by sitting here glumly,

7

making faces. I can find some if you want."

She picked up her sack and started to walk away. Velu stayed on the bench. What should he do? Should he follow this girl? Where was she going to take him? She was disappearing into the crowd, he had to make up his mind quickly. Alright, he decided. Anyway I have no idea where to go. He jumped up and ran after her. She wasn't even looking back to see where he was.

He caught up with the girl as she was leaving the station. The two of them walked to the road through the auto stand. They jumped and twisted through the vehicles, avoiding people with luggage. The girl swiped at an auto tyre with her stick as she walked by and the driver yelled at Velu. Velu was scared but the girl just started singing "*Autokaaran, autokaaran ...*" and kept walking.

When they got to the road, Velu found that the vehicles kept coming and never stopped for anyone. Smoke and dust flew at him from all sides, making his head spin. They had to wait for a long time before they could find a gap to run through. Velu kept hesitating and the girl finally dragged him to the other side.

"What do you think you're doing? Grazing cows? If you stand around in the middle of the road like that, you'll be chutney."

Velu's heart was still beating fast. He looked back at Central Station and the traffic speeding by. How had they managed to come through that? They walked along the side of the road under some huge signboards. Velu looked up at the pictures: banians, car tyres, pens, a woman holding a box. The writing was all in English, so he didn't know what they were saying.

The girl turned onto a wide bridge and walked up. Velu stopped and peeped over the railing. Under him, the road ran into the city. In the distance he could see huge buildings and towers and more roads.

"See that big building with the wall around it? If you're not careful, you'll soon be counting bars there." The girl grinned and pointed at a huge building.

Velu squinted and read the Tamil sign, *Central Jail*.

"Why? I haven't done anything."

"You don't have to do anything. Just don't get caught, that's all."

What does she mean, Velu wondered. Meanwhile the girl was already heading down the bridge with the sack on her shoulder. What was in it? He had seen her putting plastic cups into it at the station.

"What are you carrying in that bag?"

"Things. Bottles, paper."

Velu wondered what she was doing with them, but he felt shy to ask any more questions.

It was still morning but the sun blasted down on the tar and Velu's bare feet burned. It was not like walking on a mud road. He was soaked with sweat. He tried hard to walk in the shade and keep up with the girl at the same time. She walked really fast. How far away was the food?

After almost an hour of walking, they stopped in front of a big building. *Sri Rajarajeshwari Prasanna Kalyana Mandapam* read Velu slowly. A sign with letters made of flowers said, *Groom: J. V. Vinayagan, Bride: Rani*. Velu stared at the big cars parked outside. One of the cars had a flower garland and roses taped onto it. The girl looked around, pulled one off quickly and stuck it in her hair.

"Come on," she said.

"Are we going to eat here?" asked Velu, looking at the huge hall and the people inside.

"Hopes!" said the girl shaking her thumb under his nose. She led him behind the hall. There was a big garbage bin overflowing with rubbish. Two goats were standing on the pile, fighting for a banana leaf. A cloud of flies buzzed around their legs. There was a rotten smell in the air. The girl picked up a squashy banana and held it out to Velu.

"Here's your food."

Velu was shocked. "Are we going to eat their leftovers?"

"Chey! What do you think I am? A dog? I only take untouched food. Here, some more, catch!" She threw him a *vada*. Velu looked at it with distaste.

"Come on, hero, eat it! You think I like it? I told you I'll find you something to eat. Don't think I have money to buy food for you. You'd better eat what you get until you have your own money."

Velu hesitated, but his stomach squeezed him again. He gulped down the banana and vada. His stomach felt better immediately. He could have eaten at least ten times more, but the girl could find only one more banana which she ate herself.

"It's too early, they've only eaten tiffin. If you're still hungry, you'll have to wait for them to finish lunch. You can wait if you want. I have to work, I'm going." She picked up a couple of bottles from the heap and threw it into her sack. Then she walked off.

Velu panicked. He realised that if the girl left him, he had no idea where he was and what to do. It was better to stick to her, she seemed to know her way around. He ran after her again.

"Aiy!" he called. He did not even know the girl's name. "Aiy, what is your name?" he asked hurrying behind her.

She stopped and turned around. "Oho! So you've been following me around without even knowing my name. Jaya."

"I'm not following you."

"What then? Who got you food?"

"Can I come with you? Where are you going?"

"Come if you want. This bag is full, I have to go home to get another one."

Jaya and Velu walked along the roads for half an hour, until they came to a bridge across a dirty trickle of water. "We are in Triplicane now. See, that's Buckingham Canal," said Jaya.

Velu stared. This was a canal? Near some puddles of water was a row of the strangest huts he had ever seen. They were built out of all sorts of things—metal sheets, tyres, bricks, wood and plastic. They stood crookedly and looked as if they would fall any moment.

"Is this where you live? These houses are strange!" said Velu. "In our village, the houses are made of mud and palm leaves."

Jaya didn't answer and just slipped down the slope towards the huts. Velu followed her slowly. A man with a big cap walked by them with a sack on his shoulders.

"Aiy!" yelled Jaya to a group of children sitting around a huge pile of plastic bags. "Did Thomas come here in the morning?"

"No. Didn't see him. Who's this donkey you've brought?"

A few of the children nudged each other and sniggered. Velu wanted to hide from them, but he just stood next to Jaya.

"Come on."

Jaya went around to one of the huts and dumped her sack outside. Then she picked up an empty one.

"Let's go."

Houses from Trash

The next time you see one of these huts stop and look. What some people throw away as waste is valuable to others.

A thin man with a moustache came out of the hut, puffing a *bidi*. When he saw Velu, he caught Jaya by her hair.

"Who is this loafer with you?" he growled. "How many times have I told you not to pick up strays from all over the city? There's no place for anybody here."

"Oyyoyyo! Appa, let go, it hurts!" Jaya's father gave her a slap.

"I didn't bring him here, he followed me," she whined. "What can I do? Anyway, he's not going to come here for anything."

Jaya's father pushed her away and went back inside, muttering to himself. She stuck out her tongue at him.

"Pah! What does he think of himself?" she hissed. "See, all because of you."

She turned to Velu and gave him a shove. "At least help me now. Here, wear these and come with me."

She threw him a pair of old shoes without laces and pushed a sack and a stick into his hands. Velu was confused. What work did she want him to do with these things? The only work he had ever done was on the landowner's farm, weeding and taking cows out to graze.

"Are there any farms in the city?" he asked Jaya.

She laughed and thumped her stick on the ground. "Farms! There are no farmers here. We are ragpickers."

"Ragpickers?"

"See my sack? Full of things I collected."

"Collected? From where?" asked Velu.

"From rubbish bins, where else?"

"You collect rubbish?" Velu had never heard of such a thing.

"Ayye, blockhead. It's not any rubbish. Only paper, plastic, glass, metal, useful things. We sell it to Jam Bazaar Jaggu."

Velu was puzzled. He had heard of people throwing away rubbish. But why would anyone want to buy rubbish?

Ragpickers

People who sort garbage from bins and dumps are called ragpickers.

The term 'ragpicker' has an interesting history. In Europe, around two hundred years ago, textile rags were used to make paper. So some poor people began to sort rags from garbage and sell them. They came to be called ragpickers. In fact, rag smuggling was big business and the police were always on the lookout for these 'smugglers'. Over time, anyone who sorted any kind of garbage came to be known as a ragpicker.

"Who's Jam Bazaar Jaggu? Why's he buying all this?"

"You think he buys it for show? He sells it to a factory. Come on, I don't have time to waste, like you."

Velu did not move. He hadn't run away and come to this new place to dig through garbage bins. Jaya poked at him with her stick.

"Look here!" she shouted. "If someone gets there before us we won't get anything. Don't just stand there, posing. Big hero. Keep standing, what for me? I'm trying to help you. Who filled your stomach today?"

Velu scratched his head and sighed. I'll do it for now, he thought, until I find a better job.

Children at Work

Why do children work? There are many reasons— some children learn their family trade at an early age. Others, like Velu, run away from unhappy homes and have no one to look after them. They have to work to support themselves.

But most of the time children work because their families are poor. For these children, working is a necessity. They have no other choice. If their parents could earn enough money, these children would not have to work. They could go to school and play like other children of their age.

chapter two

The First Day

Jaya took Velu to a row of shops further down Buckingham Canal. They walked behind the shops to a huge rubbish bin. It was much worse than the one next to the wedding hall. Half-eaten vegetables, plastic bags, used syringes, broken bottles, cigarette packs, rusty pieces of iron and all sorts of stinking rubbish lay around the overflowing bin. Flies sat on everything and two men were using the dump as a toilet. A cow stood with its nose in the bin.

"Haiy! Haiy!" yelled Jaya, waving her stick. "Stupid cow! Eating up all the paper."

The cow wandered away. Velu watched Jaya as she poked at the garbage with her stick, sending up a buzzing cloud of flies. As soon as she turned a heap of paper over, a terrible smell rose into the air.

"Let's go somewhere else," Velu said to Jaya, holding his nose. "I can't bear it."

"You'll get used to it," said Jaya, not paying any attention to him.

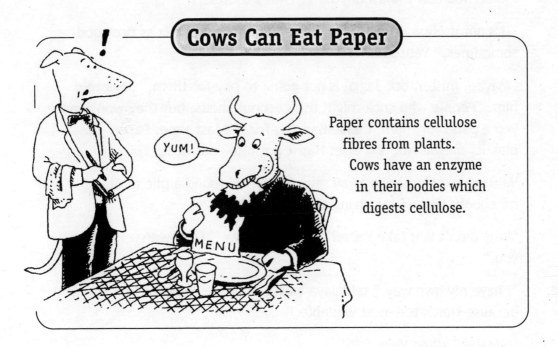

Cows Can Eat Paper

YUM!

MENU

Paper contains cellulose fibres from plants. Cows have an enzyme in their bodies which digests cellulose.

"Start searching. Only useful things—paper, plastic ... and don't expect me to give you what I find. You do your own picking."

Velu stood at the far end of the bin and poked at the rubbish with his stick. He tried to get a piece of paper, but it slipped off the stick. Jaya giggled.

"Come closer, it's not going to bite you. See, upwards, like this." She flicked up the rubbish neatly. After a few tries, Velu managed to pull a few sheets of paper out from under a pile of fruit peels.

Jaya shook her head. "No use, Jaggu never takes wet paper."

"How about this?" Velu asked, prodding some coconut shells. Jaya sighed loudly.

"Idiot! You don't know anything! That's useless."

"It's not useless. In our village, we use coconut shells as firewood sometimes," Velu said.

"Maybe, mister, but Jaggu is not going to pay for them," Jaya told him. "People who cook might use coconut shells, but they won't give you a paisa for them. I'm telling you for the last time. Paper, glass, plastic, metal. Nothing else. Has it got into your head?"

Velu pushed the shells away reluctantly. He found a pile of old notebooks tied with a string and picked them up.

"Why didn't you take these?" he asked Jaya. "They were closer to you."

"I have my own way," said Jaya with a sly look. "*Masala* first, because that's the most valuable."

"Masala?" asked Velu.

"Masala is plastic bags."

"Oh. Is this green box masala?"

"No, no, that's a juice packet. Useless."

"Aiy! Get out of here! You filthy good-for-nothings. Making a mess of the place! Out, get out."

Jaya and Velu turned around to see a shopkeeper waving a stick at them. Velu grabbed his sack and ran but Jaya stopped to pick up a few more things. The shopkeeper swung his stick and whacked Jaya on her left leg.

"Think I'm joking? Get out before you get one more."

Jaya cried out and rubbed her leg. She collected her things and limped towards Velu.

What is Recycling?

Jaya and Velu are helping to recycle things. Recycling is using things over and over or making new things out of old. It is always better to recycle than to throw things away. The things you throw away do not just disappear. They pollute the earth.

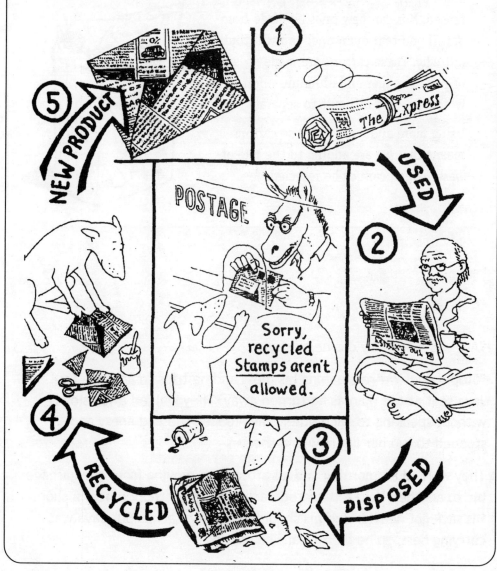

Bottles or Cartons?

When you have a cold drink from a bottle, the bottle goes back to the factory and is used again. But when you drink from a carton, you throw it away.

Some of these juice cartons cannot be reused. Nor can new ones be made from old. If you tear open one, you will find out why. These cartons are made of layers of plastic, paper and aluminium foil, which are very difficult to separate.

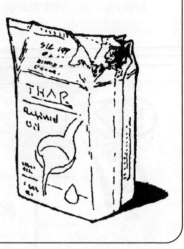

Using more and more of these cartons means that we are adding to the pile of waste which cannot be recycled.

"Are you hurt? Why did he beat you?"

"Stupid dog! We're cleaning his mess and he tries to act big. Thu!" Jaya spat at the man as he turned away. They walked away slowly without speaking to each other. Jaya looked sad and angry and stopped to rub her leg now and then.

They worked all morning and all afternoon, moving from one garbage bin to another. Velu felt scared each time they stopped near a shop. His sack got heavier and his shoulder began to ache. But Jaya was carrying hers, so he didn't dare complain.

Organic and Inorganic Wastes

The garbage bin to which Jaya took Velu is smelly, mainly because it contains organic waste. Waste matter from plants and animals is called organic or bio-degradable waste. That means it decomposes and smells. Such wastes can be composted to become fertile soil.

Wastes which do not decompose easily are called inorganic wastes. They remain on the surface of the earth for years and years.

You can do a small experiment to find out the difference between organic and inorganic wastes. Bury some pieces of glass and a few banana peels in garden soil. See which has decomposed after a week.

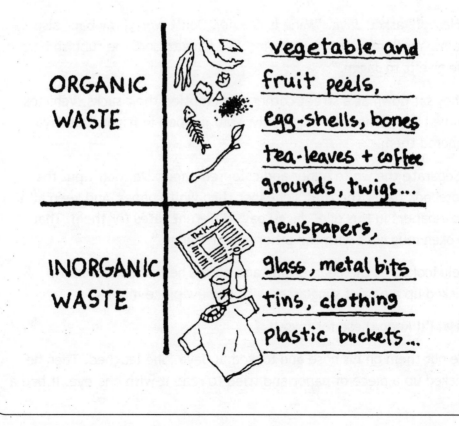

ORGANIC WASTE — vegetable and fruit peels, egg-shells, bones, tea-leaves + coffee grounds, twigs...

INORGANIC WASTE — newspapers, glass, metal bits, tins, clothing, plastic buckets...

Velu and Jaya stopped near another marriage hall late in the afternoon and found a little food in the dump there. They sat down under a tree by the side of the road and ate.

"Do you have TV in your village?" Jaya asked.

"My neighbour's shop has one. Everyone goes there to watch."

"You have brothers and sisters?"

"Two sisters, one is older than me, one is younger."

"I've got one older sister, but she's married and gone off to Chinglepet."

After they had eaten, Jaya and Velu went back to work. Their sacks were full only towards the evening and Velu was hunched over with the weight. He put his sack and rubbed his shoulder.

"Heavy?" asked Jaya. "Mine is heavier. Don't worry, my back also pains. You'll get used to it. Come, we have to sort the rubbish before we give it to Jaggu."

They sat down at a street corner and emptied their sacks. Vehicles turned the corner honking madly. Velu jumped in fright, but Jaya ignored them.

"Separate the white paper and coloured paper. No, don't put the notebook paper there. It's cheaper than white paper. And keep all the newspapers in this pile. Jaggu pays different rates for them. That broken mug goes with the other plastic things."

Velu looked at the heap of bits and pieces he had collected. He picked up a pair of sunglasses with one eyepiece missing.

"Ha! I'll keep these for myself."

He put them on his nose and looked at Jaya. She laughed. Then he picked up a piece of paper and tried to read it with one eye. It had a

picture of a gold watch on it, but Velu couldn't understand what the words said.

"Hero, leave all that. It's English, you can't read it."

"I know it's English."

"Great man. Just hurry up now."

When they had finished sorting, they put all the paper in Jaya's sack, with the masala on top. They put the other trash in Velu's sack in layers, with metal things at the bottom. Then they set off for Jam Bazaar Jaggu's shop.

Velu was really curious about Jaggu. He had even given him a name—The Ruler of Rubbish. Must be a big man, Velu thought, I've heard nothing from Jaya all day but Jaggu this, Jaggu that.

The two of them turned the corner into Pycrofts Road and entered a crowded market. Sitting on the roadside were people with huge piles of fruits. The shops were very different from the ones in Velu's village. *Amanulla Rexene Works, Babu Watch Repair, New Marriage Bedding Stores, Ibrahim Biryani Centre, Sultan Hardware*, read Velu as they walked down the road. He wondered how people could buy so much. Vehicles zig-zagged wildly through the crowd, blowing their horns. Velu found it hard to follow Jaya with the sack on his shoulder. He jumped around vendors and squeezed in between people shopping for things.

"Aiy, boy! You! Get out of the way or your head will break."

Velu looked above him. Two men were struggling to unload a huge box from the balcony of a shop onto a truck.

"Yes, you! Get lost!" one of the men shouted at him.

Velu ran towards Jaya who had gone ahead.

"What a crowded place this is!" he panted.

The Ruler of Rubbish

Jam Bazaar Jaggu, the Ruler of Rubbish, is a middleman. He buys trash from ragpickers and sells it to factories which recycle these materials into new products. Some factories, for example, make plastic buckets from old plastic.

Visit a scrap dealer in your neighbourhood. What sorts of waste does he buy? How does he sort it? Who buys waste from him?

"What do you expect? This is Jam Bazaar. It's much more crowded sometimes. Anything in the world you can get here. Look, look, that crow has stolen a bun from the bakery!"

Velu saw a man running out of his shop and waving at the sky. He laughed. "Jolly!"

"One time I saw a cow running down this road with half a jackfruit in its mouth. It couldn't see properly so it dashed a man on a scooter!" said Jaya.

"That's nothing. Once for a festival, an elephant came to our village. At night he drank up a full barrel of toddy and fell on top of the shop! They couldn't wake him up the next day."

"Wait, wait! We've walked past Jaggu's shop. There it is, next to that big drum."

The shop didn't look as big as Velu expected. It was a hut with a tin roof, perched on the side of a wide gutter. *Gandhiji Waste Mart* said a red and yellow sign hanging by the door.

A couple of bamboo poles made a bridge across the gutter. Jaya crossed over the poles and up into the shop. Velu stepped in after her.

Tilting from all sides of the small room were stacks of paper, piles of plastic, glass bottles and metal objects of all shapes and sizes. In the middle of the junk was a small clearing. In it stood the largest pair of scales Velu had ever seen. A small man wearing floppy shorts and a banian sat behind the scales. He had a big moustache and eyes that darted about as if he was searching for something. Velu stared. This was Jam Bazaar Jaggu? This was the big, powerful Ruler of Rubbish?

"Trash for you Jaggu *anna*," said Jaya, dropping her sack with a thump. She started piling her things around the scales.

"Aiy! What do you think you are doing? Don't make a mess of my shop," said Jaggu, looking bored. "And who's this little varmint you've brought?"

Without waiting for Jaya's answer, Jaggu turned away and started to weigh the garbage.

"Hmm, let's see now, it's not much," he mumbled. "One and a half kilograms of white paper, three kilos notebook paper, Tamil newspapers—two kilos, one kilo masala, six hundred grams plastic, about two kilos iron and about ten bottles." He paused.

Imported Trash

The Indian recycling industry is the biggest in the world. In fact, our recycling factories do not get enough raw materials and even buy waste plastic and paper from other countries.

Sometimes these countries also dump their unwanted trash on us. So we end up with huge amounts of poisonous and harmful wastes.

Be Indian, Buy Indian!

"Twenty rupees," he said finally, looking off into the distance.

"Twenty rupees? How?" exclaimed Jaya. "White paper is four rupees a kilogram, that comes to six rupees, plus six rupees for the notebook paper. Newspaper is another six rupees. Masala is ten rupees. And it's not ten bottles, it's fifteen. Each bottle costs fifty paisa. So that makes seven rupees fifty paisa. The iron is worth five rupees, and the plastic four rupees. The total is forty-four rupees fifty paisa. You can write it down and check if you like."

Velu stared at her, amazed at the speed at which she had calculated all this. Jaggu looked bored again.

"Don't tell me all that. The paper you brought is so dirty, I'll have to throw most of it. I'll give you thirty rupees," he muttered and counted out the money.

"Forty at least. That's also too little," Jaya wheedled.

Jaggu pulled out another four rupees. "That's all for you. If you don't like it, you can take your things back."

Jaya took the money and dragged Velu out of the shop. "Wretched dog! Always like this," she cursed when they were out on the road.

"Here, twelve rupees for you. Not bad for your first day's work. When you get better at picking, you'll get more. What do you say?"

Velu thought about the garbage bins, the flies and the smell. He looked down at the money in his hands.

"I'm hungry. Let's eat," he said.

"Now you've got some money, we can have good food," said Jaya.

She took him down Pycrofts Road and into a small lane to a teashop. *New Disco Tea Stall*, it said on the board.

Jaya and Velu spent five rupees each on buns and hot tea. It was the first real food Velu had eaten all day.

"You don't get these sweet buns in my village. Only plain ones."

"Here you get sweet buns, masala buns, plain buns, everything. But I only like sweet buns."

As they left the crowded bazaar, Velu's legs felt very heavy. It got harder to keep up with Jaya. Now that he had eaten something, all he wanted was to go to sleep somewhere. Where will I spend the night, he wondered. Jaya had said he could sleep on the pavement, but where? There was no space on the pavements as far as he could see.

"Where shall I ..." began Velu and suddenly realised that Jaya had disappeared.

He looked around but he couldn't see her anywhere. He had no idea where he was. What would he do if he lost Jaya? If she hadn't found him, he didn't know what would have happened to him. He ran up and down the street, but she was nowhere. Velu gave up. He had just sat down on the pavement when Jaya suddenly popped out from a side lane.

"Aiy! What do you think you're doing, sitting like a statue? Hurry up! I was looking for you."

"Jaya! I got scared I'd lost you."

"Lost me? Are your eyes on your bum or what? I was two feet away."

Velu hurried behind Jaya out of the market and onto a bigger road. "Where shall I sleep tonight? I can't walk anymore."

"I told you you'll have to be on the pavement near my house. You can sleep next to Arasu, I'll tell him now."

It was getting dark when they reached Triplicane. On a street corner near Buckingham Canal bridge a group of people sat around, talking and smoking. A few women cooked over small fires. Velu saw a row of bundled figures wrapped in thin bedsheets lying under a streetlight. Jaya prodded one of the smaller bundles with her toe.

"Arasu, move! Make space for one more!"

Arasu pulled the sheet off his face and blinked at Jaya and Velu.

"There's hardly enough place here as it is," he grumbled, wriggling to one side. "*Dai* Thomas. Move *da*!"

"Is that Thomas? Thomas! What about my money? You told me you'd give it today," Jaya said.

"Appappa! Can't you even let me sleep? Where am I running away? I'll give it to you in the morning. Just don't bark in my ears." He pulled his sheet tighter over his head.

"You should also look for a sheet. Otherwise the mosquitoes will kill you," Jaya said to Velu as she walked away.

Velu put his bundle down on the ground between Arasu and Thomas and rested his head on it. He was tired, but he couldn't sleep immediately.

All sorts of pictures went round and round in his head. Jaggu's moustache, Central Jail, the shopkeeper beating Jaya, the rubbish bin behind the marriage hall, New Disco Tea Stall ... what a day it had been.

Already his home and his sisters seemed so far away. What would they have thought when he didn't return home? They must be worried. I'll work really hard and save up money to send to them, he thought. He would find something to do soon. He stretched and shifted around because his arms and shoulders were paining.

"Dai! Stop kicking me and go to sleep," Thomas mumbled drowsily next to him. Velu shifted away.

He looked around at the row of sleeping figures stretched out on the pavement. What a scary thing he had done. He started to cry silently, hoping that Thomas wouldn't hear him and wake up. Finally, tired from the day, he drifted off to sleep.

chapter three

Brother

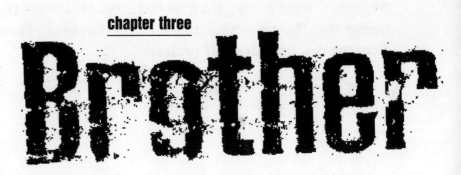

A bus roared by his ear and woke Velu early the next morning. He sat up slowly and looked around. The sky was dim and only a few bundled people were still lying on the pavement. Thomas and Arasu were gone.

Some children walked by, carrying empty buckets. Velu stood up and followed them around the corner to a pump. There was a long line of women and children with buckets and pots waiting their turn for water.

"What, great man? Come to the pump without a bucket?" Jaya was grinning at him from the middle of the queue.

Velu immediately felt at home. He walked over and stood by her. "I always wash as soon as I get up in the morning. I was coming to look for you after that."

"Wash if you want, but not here. It's corporation water, only for drinking. Go to the tap behind that house, they won't say anything."

"Alright. I'll drink here first," said Velu.

"Had tea? What happened to your remaining seven rupees?"

"Aiy! Get back here! What do you think? We're all waiting here since midnight so that you can fill water first?" A woman shouted at someone in front of her.

"Who's this, Jaya?" asked a tall girl standing behind Jaya. She looked curiously at Velu.

"Oh, this? He's Velu. He's learning from me to be a ragpicker."

The girl wrinkled her nose. "Why does he want to do that work?"

"Why not? I don't know how you wash other people's clothes and dirty vessels, day and night and say 'yes madam, no madam'," replied Jaya.

"Keep quiet. Just move up and fill your water. I have to go to work now."

"See? No free time, no movies, nothing. Look at me! If I don't feel like working, I don't. Nobody tells me what to do. Ragpicking is better. No, Velu?"

Velu didn't really think so. The thought of spending another whole day around garbage bins made him feel sick. Nobody was forcing him to work, but if he hadn't worked yesterday, he wouldn't have had the money for the buns and tea.

"It's not too bad," he said.

But that day, as he dug through one stinking bin after the other and walked in the sun with his sack, Velu wondered how long he could put up with this kind of work. By the time he and Jaya got their money from Jaggu that evening, Velu's head and body were aching.

"Fifteen rupees for you. Not bad. We were quite lucky today!" said

Jaya, tucking her money away. "Some days you can't find any masala at all."

"Oh!" said Velu. "What happens then?"

"Happens? Nothing happens. You get ten rupees or five rupees. Or even nothing some days. What mister, why the long face?"

"I'm hungry. Can we eat in the same place again?" asked Velu. "I like those sweet buns."

The two of them walked over to New Disco Tea Stall. As they were sipping their tea, two boys walked by with their arms around each other's shoulders. They looked older than Velu and Jaya. The boys stopped at the teashop and bought some matches.

"What Jaya?" one of them called out, lighting a cigarette. "New friend? Country type eh?"

"Shut your mouth Raja!" Jaya spat out. "It's not so long since you ran away from your village, so stop acting great."

"Selva and I are off to see *Arunachalam*. Rajni's superhit!" Raja boasted. "What, coming?"

Jaya just hissed and ignored him.

Velu perked up at hearing the word 'Rajni'. He suddenly forgot how tired he was. He had seen every single Rajnikanth movie which came to his village. What a hero! Super style! Nobody could bash a villain like Rajni could.

As Raja and Selva swaggered away, Velu turned to Jaya.

"Remember that scene in *Valli* where Rajni plays a guitar? Let's go to *Arunachalam* today! We have money now. That's the only Rajni film I've missed."

Jaya pulled Velu's ear. "And what will you eat tomorrow? My head?

Wait till you save some money! We can go on Friday. Come on, drink your tea. It's late."

"Late for what? Where are we going?" asked Velu, rubbing his ear.

"School."

"School! You go to school? Is that where you learnt to add so fast?"

"Yes, I am the best at maths," said Jaya.

"But how can I come with you to your school? The teacher won't let me."

"Che, che! This is not a school like that. Anyone can come and sit there."

What kind of school started in the evening? Velu followed Jaya, but his mind was still on the movie.

They walked further down Pycrofts Road, towards Marina Beach. After a while they turned into a small lane, Velu saw a short man talking to a group of children sitting on the pavement. A small girl grabbed at the man's shirt, shouting "Brother! Brother!" Three boys wrestled near the gutter. This is a school? Nobody even has a book in their hands, thought Velu.

"Brother!" Jaya shouted.

The man turned and looked at them. "What Jaya? Brought someone new?"

"Velu, Brother. He came yesterday from his village. I found him at Central and took him home."

"Why didn't you take him to our help desk? You know it is there for children like him."

Jaya shrugged. "I forgot Brother. He was hungry. I took him to eat."

"How many times have I told you not to do this?" Brother looked at the children sitting on the pavement. "All of you remember. If you meet any runaway children bring them to our help desk."

Brother turned to Velu.

"Where did you stay last night?"

"He was sleeping with us Brother," Thomas shouted.

"We have a shelter home if you want to come there for a few days. It is in T. Nagar."

"It's alright Brother, I'm there. He's learning everything from me," Jaya said.

"Which is your village?" Brother turned to Velu.

"Ponnambadi. Near Karur."

"Would you like to go back there? We can help you."

Velu shook his head.

"So what made you come to Chennai? Did you come to find work?"

Velu looked down at his feet. Some of the children were nudging each other and looking at him. He remained silent.

"Alright, Velu, we will talk more later. You can sit down. Let's start now." Brother clapped his hands. "Dasan, Arasu, Seeni! Stop that and come here!"

"How can you call this a school? No building, no flag. And the teacher doesn't have a ruler," Velu whispered to Jaya.

"I told you it's not a school like that! It's for children who work, like us," Jaya hissed back angrily. "And Brother's not a proper teacher, he's actually a priest."

"Oh, he does it to help children?"

"Yes, it's his work. Thomas says some church office sends him here."

Brother started to sing a song about working children and everybody joined in. To Velu's surprise, a tall boy next to him sang a film song loudly. Velu was sure that Brother would scold the boy, but he only said "Dasan!" and continued singing.

Jaya whispered to Velu, "Dasan works in a restaurant. See those marks on his arms? The owner beats him."

After the song, Brother passed a book to one of the children and asked him to read aloud from it.

"No reading today Brother!"

"Please, one more song."

"Thomas is tearing the book Brother!"

"Stop it! Stop it now. You might like it, but you can't sing all day. Read at least five lines each. You must learn to read properly."

"I'll read ten lines Brother!" shouted a little girl and snatched the book. She read on and on.

"Enough, enough, Ponni. Pass it on to someone else," Brother interrupted finally.

"As if she's the only one who can read. Show-off!" Jaya whispered.

When Velu finished his turn, she said "Not bad, where did you learn?"

"I liked to go to the school in my village whenever I had the time."

When everyone had finished reading, Brother distributed pencils and paper. There was not enough to go around, and two girls fought over a pencil. One of them pulled the other's hair and both started crying.

"Shoo! What is this, Devi, Selvi? No fighting and crying here. I will give chalk to those who don't have pencils and paper."

Child Labour

There are many children in India like Velu, Jaya, Thomas, Arasu and Dasan, who have to work to earn their living.

India is said to have the largest number of child labourers in the world—more than 73 million in 1997. Many of them do dangerous work such as making matchsticks and firecrackers. Others work in shops, as household servants, ragpickers, restaurant helpers, or garage assistants. These children work for low wages and are usually overworked. They have very unhealthy working environments. Often they are beaten and ill-treated by their employers.

According to the law, children below fourteen years of age are not allowed to work in factories or in any job that could be dangerous to them. But this law is often ignored. As of now, there is no law which bans child labour altogether.

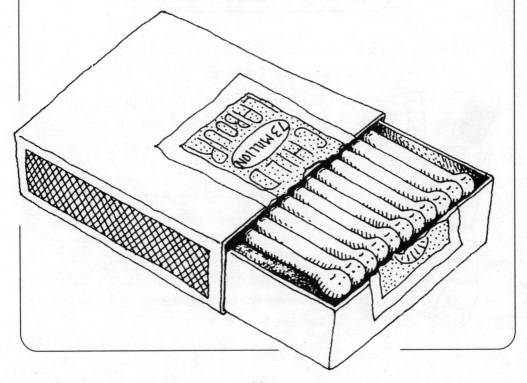

Brother passed pieces of chalk around and dictated words for them to write. Velu scribbled his words on the pavement with chalk. Dasan scribbled in the mud with a stick.

"Brother, look he's not writing, he's drawing a boat!" said a boy sitting next to him. Dasan pulled his ear and soon there was another fight. Finally even Brother's patience wore out.

"If you don't pay attention, you won't learn anything," he shouted. "What is the use of coming here and fighting? Don't you want to do well and go to proper schools later?"

Everyone became a little quieter. Then Dasan got up, dusting himself.

Writing Before Paper

Velu writes on the pavement with chalk. How did people write before paper was invented?

The Egyptians carved hieroglyphics (word pictures) on stone monuments. In India, stories about gods and kings were carved on temple walls.

Leaves were a favourite material: palm leaves in India, and olive leaves in Syracuse. Egyptians wrote on a material made from the stem of the papyrus plant. Mayans and Aztecs of South America also wrote on similar materials called Huun and Amatl.

"I have to go, Brother. Shetty *ayyah* will fire me. I can't fill my stomach with alphabets." He walked away slowly.

As it got later, more children got up and left. Some had to work in the evening, others had to walk a long way home. Jaya and Velu stayed till the end.

"You read well, Velu. You should come regularly with Jaya," Brother called out to them as they left.

On their way back, Velu said "Nice school. Why don't Raja and Selva come? And your friend at the pump this morning?"

"Lakshmi has no time. She has to look after her small brothers after work. Raja and Selva? No chance! Stay away from them, they're no good. They work for Dorai."

School or Work?

Not everybody went to school in the olden days. In Europe it was the children of the wealthy, or those wanting to be priests or teachers who went to school. In India, only the male children of upper caste or wealthy families were educated. The children of the poor or the lower castes learned the trade of their forefathers.

During the early nineteenth century, in Europe, the idea evolved that all children, rich or poor, should go to school, so that they had a choice of professions as adults.

In India too there are laws which say children should not be forced to work but should be in school instead. Unfortunately these laws are not followed.

"Dorai? Who's he? Does he buy garbage, like Jaggu?" asked Velu.

"Che, no! He doesn't buy anything. He deals in money. Just keep away from Dorai and those two. Don't talk to them."

Schools for Working Children

Today there are many organisations which run pavement schools of the kind Jaya and Velu go to. These schools aim to improve working children's lives by teaching them reading, writing and arithmetic.

However some people argue that going to school will not help these children earn a living. It would be better instead to train a working child in a particular skill, like carpentry, tailoring, welding, or electrical work.

Learning a skill is good, but not just for working children. All children would benefit from it. Likewise, basic schooling is essential for all children.

The lives of working children can change permanently only when they do not have to work for a living.

chapter four

Bungalow Houses

The next morning Jaya took Velu to a different part of the city. Instead of going towards Central station, they walked in the other direction, towards Mylapore. At Luz Corner, she stopped outside the Vinayagar temple.

"Just wait. This is a good place."

Velu sat by the side of the temple wall and looked around. A few other children were sitting there as well. Soon a man and woman drove up in a new car.

"Get ready! These people have come to do puja for their car."

A priest came out of the temple and greeted the couple.

"See him? I've seen him riding on a scooter. He lives in Triplicane."

The priest said some prayers. He put *kumkum* on the doors and walked round and round the car ringing a bell. Finally, he held up a coconut and broke it on the road. All the waiting children jumped on the scattered pieces.

"Dai, Muruga! Come, there's lots here."

"Give me a piece da! Give me a piece da!"

"Jaya, look! I got half the coconut." Velu crawled out from under the car.

"Put it under your shirt you fool. Quickly! Let's go."

Jaya and Velu walked along, chewing on the coconut pieces. Ten minutes later they reached Mylapore. Near the Kapaleeshwarar temple gate they looked around and found a piece of sugarcane and half a cucumber.

Then they walked around the huge temple tank and down the side streets, past stalls stuffed with fruits and vegetables. There was hardly any plastic in the bins there, only heaps of banana stalks and rotten vegetables. Cows moved from bin to bin, eating up whatever they could find.

"This garbage smells different," said Velu. "A bit like manure."

"Don't bother with this place. We'll find better things on the other side."

Jaya took Velu through a maze of tiny lanes, turning left and right and jumping out of the way of trolleys and cycle rickshaws.

"Look! Just look there," Velu pointed and laughed.

"Stop! Aiy, you! Stop. My cap!" A man in a rickshaw shouted loudly to the man pedalling it. The wind had lifted the man's cap and put it on the balcony of a house.

Jaya and Velu watched the man trying to get his cap back until they had to move aside for a bullock cart. They turned into a narrower street. The doors of the houses were right on the road and all sorts of smells came floating out from them—coffee, turmeric, chilli powder. In the bins around these houses Jaya and Velu found some plastic bags, bulbs and a few broken mugs. Then they walked on through the streets away from the temple.

"See that big tree? Sometimes a man sits there with a cobra in a basket. That cobra is twice as long as you and he plays music to it."

"That's nothing, there's a cobra bigger than that living near the well in my house," said Velu.

After half an hour of walking, they came to a place with shady, quiet roads and big bungalows. There were only five or six houses on a street, and they all had compound walls and a watchman standing at the gate. The road was swept and there was a huge garbage bin at the corner.

Do All Indians Generate the Same Amount of Trash?

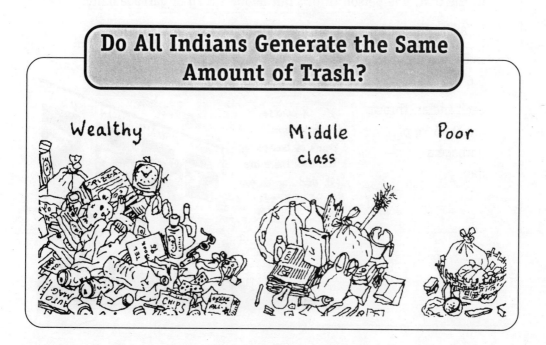

Wealthy

Middle class

Poor

"What will we get here? There are so few houses on this street!" Velu asked, puzzled.

"Just wait, you won't believe what all these bungla houses throw away," Jaya said.

The More You Have, the More You Throw Away

Wealthy people throw out more trash than poor people. It is the same with countries. Some countries are considered more developed than others. People there use more goods produced by machines and there are fewer poor people. The average person has more of everything: more food, more clothes, more cars. They also generate more trash.

In the USA, one person throws out about 1.8 kg of garbage daily.

In Australia, each person throws out about 1.6 kg of garbage.

In Japan, one person throws out 0.6 kg.

Each Indian throws out 0.46 kg of garbage a day.

It was true. In the bin, Velu discovered ice cream cups, shoes, plastic shampoo bottles, toys, even an old clock and a broken transistor.

"Careful," Jaya said when she saw Velu holding up the cover of a tin can. "That'll cut your hand in half."

They spent a long time picking up things from the bin.

Convenient Trash

We produce more waste today than we did ten years ago, because there are many more products available in the market, to be used briefly and then thrown away. People buy disposable paper plates, plastic spoons, or paper tissues simply because they are convenient.

But what happens to these things when we are finished with them? Where do they go?

What is convenient for us can be extremely damaging to the environment. We make life easier for ourselves at the cost of making the world ugly and unhygienic.

No hassles!

Reducing Rubbish

Check your household garbage for one day. Separate and compost organic waste. Look through the inorganic rubbish. Some of it can be recycled or reused either by you or by others. You will find that a lot of trash is simply of no use to anyone and is harmful to the environment.

The amount of inorganic waste we throw away today is huge. We prefer to buy things which are wrapped in fancy packages. Though all packaging creates waste, some kinds are more harmful than others.

It may not be possible for you to not create trash at all. But you can think a little, and use things which are less harmful for the environment. For example, if you are packing food to carry, use a box which you can wash out again. If you cannot carry an empty box around for some reason, it is best to use banana leaves, since they are organic matter. If you cannot find them, use aluminium foil, which you can wash and reuse. Try to avoid throw-away plastic bags.

REDUCE-ABLE
REUSE-ABLE
RECYCLE-ABLE
COMPOST-ABLE

"Jaggu won't take many of these things, but we can use them at home," Jaya said. "Try these shoes, they look big enough. You can throw your old ones away." The shoes were a little too loose, but Velu decided to keep them.

"What is this box?" asked Velu.

"That's not a box, you dolt. It's Pepsican, for cool drinks."

Suddenly Jaya bundled up her bag and pulled Velu's hand. "Run, police car!"

A white jeep with a blue light on the roof was driving slowly along.

"Why should we run? We haven't done anything."

"Shut up idiot, just run."

Jaya let go of Velu and disappeared round the corner. Velu followed her. The two of them ran until they came to the traffic lights on the main road.

"What will the police do, Jaya?"

"What will they do?! Lock you up and beat you!"

"But why?"

"Who knows? You know what happened to Thomas? Once he found a necklace in a bin near T. Nagar. Stupid fool took it to the police. You know what they did? Locked him up and said he had stolen it. They thrashed him so badly he couldn't walk for weeks!"

"But we didn't go to them, we were just working."

"You think they care? Ragpickers or thieves or pickpockets, it's all the same to them. Just run if you see police, don't wait around."

That evening they didn't get much money from Jaggu, but Velu felt good slapping around in the shoes he had found.

New Disco Tea Stall was closed, so they bought boiled eggs from a woman in Triplicane. Velu thought about buying some buns, but he decided to save his money for a movie.

"Don't forget tomorrow's Friday. We're going to *Arunachalam*," Velu reminded Jaya as they came near her house.

"Who forgets? You'll forget, not me." She ran down the embankment.

Velu lay down on the pavement with mosquitoes buzzing in his ears. I must get a sheet soon, he thought, covering his face with his hands. But he fell asleep quickly, dreaming of the movie they were going to see the next day.

Asking for Protection

Jaya is afraid of the police. But in fact, she has the right to ask the police to protect her. In a democratic country like India, every citizen has certain rights.

A right is something you are entitled to. For example, you are entitled to ask your government to protect you from violence, help you live in good health and to allow you to say what you think.

These rights are the same for everyone, whether man or woman, child or adult, rich or poor. But the rights of poor children like Velu are often disregarded.

Some Important Rights that Every Child Has

The governments of many countries in the world have agreed that children have some important rights. It is the duty of the government to make sure that these rights are given to children:

1. The right to life. Every child that is born must grow up into a healthy adult.

2. The right to be protected from violence. No child should be ill-treated or neglected. Even if the parents or guardians of a child treat her badly, the government can interfere and stop them from doing so.

3. The right to education. Primary education should be compulsory and available to everyone. All children should attend school regularly.

4. The right to rest and leisure. All children should be able to play and have the chance to do other things like sing, dance, paint or act.

5. The right to express themselves. Every child has the right to ask for information and to give information if she wants to.

6. The right to be protected from exploitation. Children should not be taken away from schools and forced to do work which harms their health and growth.

City Life

chapter five

Over the days Velu learned how to be a ragpicker. He and Jaya
worked together, setting out early every morning with a fixed
routine.

On Mondays they went to Central station and along Anna Salai. On
Tuesdays they searched the bins near Ice House and Parthasarathy
temple. On Wednesdays they went to Mylapore. They picked garbage
outside the markets and shops near Jam Bazaar on Thursday.

Friday and Saturday they worked during the day in Royapettah and
set out again late at night to collect bottles from bars and wine
shops. On those days they managed to make a little more money, but
it was hard to keep awake the next day, so they only went out at
night twice a week. Sundays they worked all evening along Marina
Beach, picking up things the Sunday crowds threw away.

Sometimes, if they were not too tired, Velu and Jaya stayed back at
the beach till everyone had left. Close to midnight when the beach

was empty and there was no one to shoo them away, they went to the playground and played on the ladders and the slide. They climbed and ran around until they were too tired to play any more. Then they walked home, with sand in their hair and clothes.

As the days went by, Velu's home felt further and further away. It was almost as if he had been living in Chennai for years and not just weeks. But most nights, when Velu lay down on the pavement, he thought of his home and his sisters. On days that he earned a little more, he thought of how they would feel if he suddenly returned to his village with nice clothes for them. On days that he earned nothing and had to go hungry, he wondered whether he would ever see them again.

When Velu first came to Chennai he thought it was a huge place with a lot of strange new things to see. He had been scared but also excited. He hadn't been sure about what he would find, but he had thought he could find a way to make money. Now he knew that he had to work all day just to get enough food to last him for the next one.

Every day felt like the other and it never seemed to end. He had to get up early in the morning even if he had worked late the previous night. He had to pick up his sack and his stick and he had to walk the same streets looking out for garbage. He knew every garbage bin in Triplicane, he knew Pycrofts Road and Jam Bazaar and Mylapore.

Now and then, Velu wondered if he should find other work. Should he clean tables in a restaurant? But Dasan worked in a restaurant and he was beaten everyday by the owner. And Dasan's friend who worked in a garage said his boss thrashed him even if he was ten minutes late. So Velu continued to be a ragpicker. At least I have a friend like Jaya, he thought.

The only time Velu did something different was when he attended his school on Tuesday evenings. He enjoyed reading and singing with

Brother, and he liked to scribble things on paper. Each time he came back from school, Velu would promise himself that he would work harder at reading and writing, but he never found the time to practice. He hardly did anything but ragpicking.

The one thing Velu and Jaya never missed was their movie on Friday evenings. All week they saved up their money for the movie, trying to put aside two rupees everyday so that they had ten rupees for their ticket by Friday. On Friday nights, Velu always had happy dreams.

chapter six

Trapped

One Wednesday evening Jaya and Velu finished work early because it started drizzling. The rubbish in the bins was so soggy that they earned almost nothing that day.

Jaya ran home from Jaggu's shop in the rain, but there was no shelter near his pavement so Velu sat huddled under the roof of New Disco Tea Stall. He wondered where he would sleep that night if the rain didn't stop.

"Oy, Velu! What da, all alone? Where's your bodyguard?" Velu looked up to see Raja and Selva grinning at him.

"She's gone home," he replied, not looking at them.

"Why are you sitting here in this place? Come with us, we're going for a movie." Raja winked at Selva.

"I only go to the movies on Fridays. Who has the money to just come with you?"

"Oh, money? Don't worry about that, I'll pay for your ticket and all," offered Raja.

Velu was puzzled.

"Why do you want to pay for me?"

"See him Selva, we want to be his friend and he's so suspicious. Is this the way to behave?"

Velu hesitated. He remembered Jaya's warning to stay away from the two boys.

"I won't come without Jaya," he said finally.

"If you want to come, you better come fast. The movie starts in half an hour. It's *Padayappa*, Rajnikanth's latest. That's all I can say," Raja added.

He started walking away. Selva followed.

Velu didn't know what to do. Why were they calling him and paying for his ticket? They weren't his friends, and Jaya had said they were no good.

But they were calling him for a Rajni movie, free! He wouldn't have to work all week to save for it. He didn't feel like going back to sleep on a wet pavement. What was the harm in going to a movie? Velu got up suddenly.

"Aiy! Wait for me. I'm coming," he shouted.

Velu enjoyed the movie fully. It was such a treat, that too on a day when he had been feeling miserable. He leaned back in his seat, stuck his legs out and watched. All his worries went out of him.

When he came out he felt fresh and happy.

"Super! What a dance scene no, da?" he said to Selva when they were on the street.

It had stopped raining. The three of them walked down the road with their arms around each other's shoulders, talking about the film.

"Ha! Yes, which heroine did you like better?" Selva asked.

"Ramyakrishnan. You?"

"Same da. She's the best."

"Did you see Sivajiganesan?"

"Sivajiganesan? One time he was great da. Now he comes for two minutes and goes."

"So? What Velu? Suppose you hadn't come with us?" Raja grinned.

Velu was glad that he had gone along. These two weren't as bad as Jaya said they were.

Raja took them to a push-cart selling food and bought Selva and Velu a grand meal of *parottas* and egg curry. When they had eaten, Selva went to a shop and bought cigarettes.

"Here, smoke one. It's great!" He gave Velu a cigarette. Velu had seen Thomas and Dasan smoke cigarettes and bidis, but he had never tried it himself.

"No da, I don't want it."

"Come on, what's this?"

"Watch!" said Raja. He tossed a cigarette up in the air and caught in his mouth. Exactly like Rajnikanth.

"Can you do that?" he challenged Velu.

Why not, Velu thought. I'll try it once and see. He threw a cigarette in the air and opened his mouth. It hit his nose and fell down on the ground. He tried it again. After the fifth try, he managed to catch it.

"Super, da!" applauded Raja. "But you've made chutney of this cigarette. Here, have another."

He lit a cigarette and passed it to Velu. Velu puffed on it and coughed. He didn't like it much, it made his head buzz.

"Like it?" asked Raja.

Velu nodded. Raja and Selva led such different lives—movies everyday, good food!

"How do you have so much money?" he asked them.

The two boys smiled at each other.

"Dorai anna gave it to us. He pays much more than anyone else. If you want money he'll give you too. We'll speak to him. How much do you need?"

Velu was about to say "Hundred rupees," when he remembered what Jaya had said. He shook his head.

"No, no, I don't want any."

"Come on, da! Who doesn't want money? Just think, we can go to a movie again tomorrow. *Rajasthan* is going on at Santham theatre. Everyday you can eat well." Raja started humming "*Padayappa, padayappa ...*"

Velu thought about the evening. It was true, this was the best time he had had since he ran away from home.

"So, want to go and see Dorai anna?" Raja asked, breaking off in the middle of the song.

Velu began to shake his head, when suddenly a thought struck him. If he took some money from Dorai, he could send it to his sisters. He was ready to do whatever work Dorai asked him to do for it. They would be so surprised to get the money. He imagined the excitement when the postman delivered his money-order. He hadn't even written to his sisters to say he was alright. Now he could really show them what he had done.

"Alright," he said finally.

"Come on then, let's go."

"What? Now? Won't he be sleeping?"

"Sleeping? Dorai anna? Don't worry. He'll be there."

As they walked towards Dorai's place, Velu's stomach tightened. Now he wished he hadn't asked for the money. What would Dorai make him do for it?

Raja and Selva took Velu back to Pycrofts Road. It was emptier than usual and most of the shops had closed for the night. Some small stalls and restaurants were still open. Raja stopped outside Murali Cafe.

"Wait on the steps, I'll call him."

Velu stood outside and peeped in. He saw Raja walking up to an enormous man dressed in a white dhoti and shirt. Raja said something to him and the man got up from the table, yawning. As he came closer, Velu noticed that he was wearing a big gold watch and a gold chain.

"Ahh, so this is the boy. What is your name?"

Dorai was really huge. He filled up the doorway of Murali Cafe.

"Velu." It came out in a whisper.

"What's that? Jayu?"

"Velu, Dorai anna. His name is Velu," Raja put in.

"Hmm. So, Raja tells me you need some money. How much?"

Velu didn't know what to say. He looked at the ground and scratched his head.

"What is this? You don't know how much you need? Hundred? Two hundred? Three hundred?" Dorai raised his voice.

Velu's head was spinning. Three hundred?!

"Say something! Dorai anna will get angry otherwise. Say hundred or two hundred. You asked me to bring you here and now you're keeping quiet," Raja hissed.

"Hundred," Velu found himself saying.

"Hundred? That's all? Alright, here." Dorai shoved two fifty rupee notes in Velu's face.

"Wh ... what will I have to do for it?" Velu asked. He couldn't believe it. He asked for hundred and Dorai gave it to him just like that.

Dorai laughed and slapped Velu on the shoulder. "Do? Do, he says. Nothing to do. Just go and enjoy yourself with these boys and give me back the money in one week. With the usual interest."

"Interest? I ... I don't want this," Velu stammered, suddenly realising what all this meant.

"Dai!" growled Dorai grabbing Velu by his shirt. "Why did you come here, then? Think I have time to waste? Want me to give you a nice thrashing?" He lifted his hand.

Velu cowered and held his hands over his head. Dorai turned to Raja.

"How dare you two bring an idiot like this to me?"

"Leave him anna! We'll talk to him." Raja pulled Velu away from the door and dragged him down the stairs.

"Fool! Talking to Dorai anna like that! You're lucky we saved you from a beating," Raja said.

"You never told me about paying interest. I thought I had to do work for Dorai anna."

"Shows what a fool you are," Selva said.

"I won't take this money. You give it back to him." Velu tried to push the money into Raja's hands.

"Are you mad? He'll kill us," Selva said.

"We try to help you and you behave like this!" Raja spat. "Just take the money and pay Dorai anna next Tuesday. With interest you have to pay him back one hundred and fifty rupees."

"Where will I get so much money? I can't do it!" Velu pleaded.

"That's your problem da. Now get lost." Raja pushed Velu away.

"And remember, even if you return the money to Dorai anna today, you still have to pay one hundred and fifty." Selva added slyly.

Velu was stunned. What had he got himself into? Just a few hours ago, these boys had been so nice, spending money on him. Now he saw why they had done it. Jaya said they worked for Dorai. This was their work! She was right, they were no good.

He clutched the hundred rupees in his hands and ran down Pycrofts Road. His heart beat loudly. What was he to do? I mustn't tell Jaya about this, he thought. She'll kill me for sure.

The next day it rained again. The garbage bins were flooded, and Velu and Jaya could not work. They managed to find a few bottles but everything else was a mess. Velu couldn't sleep on the pavement in the rain, so he took shelter near Chepauk station. It was crowded with other people from the pavement and there was hardly any dry place to sleep.

When it was time for dinner, he had no money left. He felt the two fifties in his pocket and hesitated. He was really hungry. I'll spend a little of Dorai's hundred, he thought. What's the use of keeping it in my pocket all the time?

The rain stopped late that night and on Friday Velu and Jaya could go out and work again. But neither of them had saved any money that week.

"Forget about the movie da. No money!" Jaya grimaced.

Velu was tempted to use a little more of the money he had got from Dorai. But he decided that he couldn't risk spending any more of the eighty-five that he had left. Besides, how could he explain to Jaya where he had got it?

So, for the first time, they missed their Friday movie.

chapter seven

Pay Up!

Jaya and Velu worked all weekend to make up for the time they had lost because of the rains. On Sunday Velu didn't eat anything, he only drank tea, thinking he could save the money to pay back Dorai.

But by Monday evening he still had only a hundred rupees. Velu put the money in a plastic packet and pinned it inside the pocket of his shorts. Three times that evening he counted and re-counted his money, hoping that somehow there would be more. But it always came to a hundred rupees.

He sat on the pavement with a hollow feeling in his stomach. Dorai had almost beaten him for not taking the money. What would he do to him if he didn't pay it back? When Velu finally managed to sleep, the sky was already getting lighter.

"Dai, Velu!"

Someone shook his shoulders.

"Ayyo!" Velu yelled and shot up. "Don't hit me! I'll give you your money back." He covered his face with his hands.

"What? Money eh? What are you shouting da?" Jaya grinned at him.

"Oh, you. Why do you shout like that? I had a bad dream."

"Enough dreaming, Maharaja. We have work to do."

Velu pulled himself up. Tuesday! Unless some miracle happened before evening, he was finished. Dorai would be sitting in Murali Cafe, waiting for him.

Wild thoughts of running away from Chennai came into his head. But if he ran away, Dorai might send the police to find him. What then? He would be caught and beaten by both.

As they picked through the bins that day, Velu's head felt heavy. He kept looking this way and that, in case he saw Dorai or Raja and Selva.

"Aiy, sleepy face. Are you blind or what? You're picking up all sorts of junk today. Look properly or you'll only get five rupees," Jaya prodded Velu.

Velu couldn't think clearly. He wished he could tell Jaya what was on his mind. But she'll only shout at me, he thought. And anyway, nobody can help me now.

As they neared Pycrofts Road that afternoon, Velu's heart began to beat faster.

"Jaya, shall we go to Jaggu's shop through that side lane? Why always go on Pycrofts Road?"

"What? Why da? That's such a long route, this way is the best."

Jaya turned into Pycrofts road. Velu dragged himself behind her. When they came near Murali Cafe, Velu's eyes darted to see if Dorai was there. Luckily there was a big van parked in front of the entrance. Velu crept around the van and ran on. He had managed to get past Murali Cafe, he was safe!

At the corner, he turned to see if Jaya was following him. Suddenly two arms grabbed him from behind.

"What da? Where are you going? Dorai anna has been asking about you."

Velu wriggled around, pushing the arms away. It was Raja. They had found him.

"It seems you have some money for Dorai anna." Raja held Velu by his collar.

"Aiy Raja! Let him go!" Jaya ran up, pulling Velu away. "What has he done?"

"Mind your own business. Do you know what your great friend has done? I'm sure he didn't tell you he took a hundred rupees from Dorai anna."

"I'll give it back, I'll give it!"

"What? Hundred rupees?! You never told me all this. Idiot!"

"He was supposed to give it today. Where is it da?" shouted Raja.

"Just leave him. How much does he owe now?" Jaya stood between Raja and Velu.

"Hundred and fifty."

"Dai, Velu! You've gone and spent everything? On what?"

"No, no! I have hundred rupees in my pocket."

"Alright. Give it to him," said Jaya. "You can tell Dorai anna he'll have the rest by tomorrow."

"You go tell him that. Get the beating instead of me," Raja replied, not taking the money from Velu.

"Take it! He'll give you the rest tomorrow," Jaya insisted. "I'll see that he does."

"How?" Raja asked suspiciously. "You'll give it?"

"Why do you worry who gives what? You'll get fifty rupees tomorrow, that's all. What? You won't take even my word? Who helped you when you were in trouble?"

"Alright," said Raja suddenly. "But not fifty rupees. He has to pay interest for one more week. Now he owes Dorai anna another hundred. I'm doing it only because of you. If anna doesn't get the cash this week ... finished! Tell him what happened to Dasan." Raja walked away quickly.

"Stupid fool!" Jaya hit Velu on the head. "This is what you go and do behind my back? How many times did I tell you to keep away from those two?"

"But they tricked me Jaya!"

"Who asked you to even talk to them? How did it happen?"

Velu told her the whole story. He felt better that she finally knew everything, even if she was angry with him. After all, Jaya had saved him for the moment. Still, where would he get the money to pay Dorai tomorrow?

"Leave it now," said Jaya finally. "Let's just finish with Jaggu quickly and go to school."

"And tomorrow?"

"We'll think of something later. That's a long way off."

Velu didn't think so, but he trailed behind Jaya. At school he didn't

pay much attention to what was going on. He didn't even feel anything when Brother said that there was a surprise for them the next morning.

"Velu! What did I say? No need to worry," Jaya said as they walked home.

"Eh? What?" He was still lost in thought.

"Didn't you hear? Brother said we've all been called to a workshop tomorrow. Dorai will never find you there."

"What's a workshop?" Velu asked.

"Brother says some people will come and ask us questions about ragpicking."

"Why do they want to know?"

"I don't know. I went to one before where they made us draw."

"Why?"

"Why? Why? How do I know? Just enjoy. They'll give us food and all. No work! Want to come or not?"

"I'll come, I'll come," said Velu.

Normally he would have been excited about it, but the only thing he could think about was to escape from Dorai.

That night he had a strange dream. Dorai chased him through an empty theatre. *Padayappa* ran on the screen. Suddenly Rajnikanth stepped out of the screen, wearing a suit of fifty rupee notes. He gave Dorai a good thrashing. Then he took Velu with him and made him a famous film star.

chapter eight

Clean or Dirty

Everyone gathered at the pavement school early that morning. Arasu and Thomas were there, as well as some other children Velu had not seen before. Brother took them all to the bus stop near Bells Road.

"Our bus number is 13B. When it comes, no pushing. Go in one at a time. Nobody should stand near the door."

As soon as 13B arrived, everyone rushed in, pulling each other and shouting.

"Dai Velu! Let's go right to the front and see how it looks."

"I want to buy the tickets Brother! Give me the money."

"Aiy, super da! What speed." Arasu hung out of the door.

"I will buy the tickets for everybody. Arasu! Come back inside. It is dangerous! Stop that and sit down quietly," Brother raised his voice.

The conductor shouted at Arasu and dragged him in. Then Arasu and

Thomas hung from the railing, singing *"Autokaaran, autokaaran"*.

Brother looked relieved when they finally got off the bus at Pondy Bazaar.

"Come, come, Seeni. You can't stay on the bus. Prabhu! Don't cross the road, we have to go this way."

Brother herded the children down Thiyagaraja Road and into the compound of a housing colony. There was a playground with swings, slides and see-saws in the grounds. The children rushed towards it.

"Not now, not now! They're waiting for us in that house. You can all play later."

Brother finally managed to drag everyone to the house. Velu read the sign over the door: *Anbu Illam-House for Working Children*. As soon as they stepped inside, the children fell silent. Velu looked around.

It was a big room with mats on the floor. There were posters and a blackboard on the wall. Two women stood near the blackboard. Velu knew one of them, she sometimes taught at the pavement school. Brother went over to them, wiping his face with a handkerchief.

"What is this place, Jaya?" whispered Velu.

"Brother works here. It is a home for children like us."

"What do they do here?"

"We can stay in this place for some time. Remember, the first time you came to school, Brother said you could stay here?"

"Alright children. Everybody sit in a circle. We will begin as usual with our song."

After the song Brother stood up and introduced the two women. "This is Bina *akka*, she is a teacher. She has come once or twice to our school. And this is Viji akka, she is part of a group that helps to keep our city clean. She is very interested in your work. Some of you have been in workshops before, but many of you may be wondering what we will be doing here for the next three days. We will start ..."

"Three days!" Velu whispered to Jaya. "I can escape from Dorai for three days!"

"Ha! He won't even know where we've gone."

"Do Raja and Selva know this place?"

"Yes, but they won't dare to come here."

"Why? Will Brother beat them?"

"Chah! Nobody gets beaten here. Those two ran away from this place and started working for Dorai. That's why."

At the word 'Dorai' Velu's stomach grew smaller. Suddenly he had a horrible thought. "But if we don't work for three days, where will I get hundred rupees?"

Jaya nudged him. "Shhh. Brother's looking."

"... so that you know more about your own work. And so that you understand how important it is for you to study and have a better life," Brother was concluding, looking straight at them. Velu realised he had missed most of the speech.

Thomas spoke up. "There is nothing to know about our work, Brother. We just pick up what other people throw away."

"But if you don't pick it up, what would happen to the garbage? Where would it go?" Viji akka asked them.

"It would just lie there, that's all," Jaya said.

"Really? Would it lie there? Or would something happen to it?" Viji akka asked again.

No one answered.

"What would happen if you didn't go to the bins? Arasu, why don't you say?" Brother prompted.

"Cows would eat it."

"All of it?" asked Viji akka.

"Only the food akka," Ponni corrected.

"Even the paper!" Jaya put in.

"And the rest of the things would be taken away by the corporation lorry," added Seeni.

"But taken where? What would happen to them then?" Viji akka asked.

"They throw it in a big heap near Pallikaranai akka! My sister lives there," said a girl next to Velu.

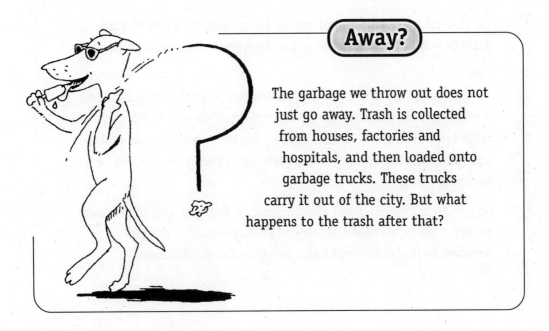

Away?

The garbage we throw out does not just go away. Trash is collected from houses, factories and hospitals, and then loaded onto garbage trucks. These trucks carry it out of the city. But what happens to the trash after that?

What Should We Do with Garbage?

As of now we dispose of most garbage either by dumping or burning it.

Trash is dumped on empty pieces of land, called landfills. Some of this garbage contains poisonous waste from factories, which pollutes not only the land, but also underground water.

We also try to get rid of garbage by burning it. It is bad to burn garbage—it pollutes the air, and is dangerous for people to breathe in.

We have to think of better ways to dispose of waste. As individuals, we can help by reducing the amount of trash we add to what is collected in the city—by composting organic wastes in our homes and neighbourhoods, and consciously using things which can be recycled.

At the same time, citizens should demand that the city corporation work out better ways of disposing of garbage which cannot be recycled, so that it does not harm people or the environment.

"That's right. But what happens after they throw everything there? Things like vegetables and food which grow from the soil become manure after some time. They go back to the soil again."

"Yes akka! My sister feeds all that to the pumpkin plants," Velu spoke up for the first time.

"Oh, do you come from a village?"

"Yes akka, Ponnambadi."

"But here in the city there are many more things like bottles, plastic bags and cans that can't become part of the soil. They just stay as they are, for years and years. So if you didn't pick up these things, they would just be lying in heaps everywhere."

Velu thought about heaps of trash covering houses and trees. If they didn't pick it up, people would have to walk up and down hills of rubbish to go anywhere.

"Alright. Let's play a quick game," Viji akka said. "Why don't you all go out now, and bring in some garbage. Not too much ..."

At the thought of going out, everyone jumped up.

"What will you do with it akka?"

"This room will smell bad!"

"When we go out, Thomas will run away akka."

"When will you give us tea?"

Viji akka looked helplessly at Brother. He stood up and knocked on the blackboard with a duster.

"Quiet! Quiet everyone. What is this noise? Akka wants to show you something. Now go out and be back within ten minutes. I will give you plastic bags to put things in. Each of you take one as you go out."

They were soon back with their collection.

"Now get together in groups of four and make a pile of what you have collected. Then sort it out the way you do for scrap-dealers," Viji akka said.

"What's a scrap-dealer?" Velu asked Jaya.

"Like Jaggu, idiot."

The Formal and Informal Waste Disposal System

The government gets rid of waste in the cities through a formal— or official—system of cleaning the streets and removing garbage. But in most cities, garbage remains in huge, nasty piles at street corners and roadsides.

In India we also have an informal system of waste disposal through ragpickers who are not paid by the government, but work on their own. Can the formal and informal systems work together?

To do this, we need to understand and value ragpicking. Ragpickers actually recycle garbage. This is important work, so they need to be paid better. Their status in society should also change. It should not be restricted to certain castes, and should not be done by children.

Ragpickers are forced to sift through rotting wastes which exposes them to injury and illness. They need protection like gloves and masks. At the same time, the garbage they sort through should not contain poisonous or harmful things.

Velu wanted to be in Jaya's group, but he found himself with Thomas and two girls he didn't know.

"Aiy! Come on, let's be first," one of the girls pulled at Velu.

They put white paper in one heap, newspaper in another and plastic in a third. Thomas had some iron pieces which they kept separately. They added a mug to the other plastic things. Broken glass, bottles, bulbs and rubber pieces went into a small pile.

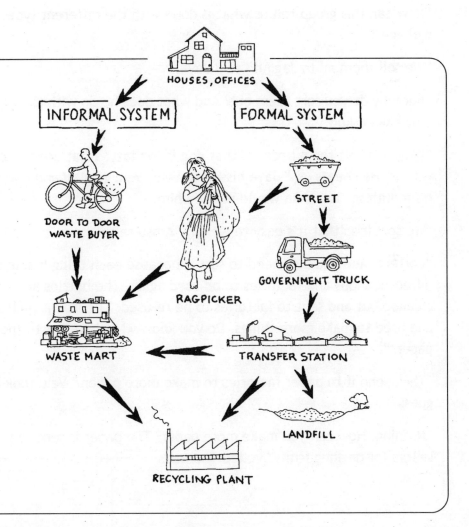

HOUSES, OFFICES

INFORMAL SYSTEM

FORMAL SYSTEM

DOOR TO DOOR
WASTE BUYER

RAGPICKER

STREET

GOVERNMENT TRUCK

WASTE MART

TRANSFER STATION

RECYCLING PLANT

LANDFILL

Once they had finished, Velu looked around to see what the others were doing. Suddenly he felt strange to be sitting in a big room, doing what he normally did by the side of the road in Triplicane.

"Finished akka! What now?" Thomas said.

"That was quick!" Viji akka looked surprised. "You're really experts at this."

"What, Jaya? We sort much bigger piles everyday. This is nothing!" Velu leaned across and whispered. Still, he felt pleased to be called an 'expert'.

"Now can this group tell us what is done with the different types of garbage?"

"We sell them all to Jaggu!" said Jaya.

"But why do you sort them out? And what does he do with them?" Bina akka asked.

"Why? We sort them because that dog is too lazy. What does he do with it? He cheats us," Jaya hissed to Velu. Velu giggled and covered his mouth so that akka would not see him.

"We sort it so that it's easy to weigh," Arasu said.

"Correct. And you also need to sort it because each thing is sold to different shops and factories to be used again. The bottles are cleaned out and sent to factories to be re-used. The iron is melted and used to make more things. Do you know what happens to the paper?"

"They send it to paper factories to make more paper." Velu took a guess.

"Nothing. How can you make more paper? The paper is sent to fruit-sellers for packing fruit," yelled Thomas.

"Keep quiet da! They make paper bags with it. Those women near my house make them everyday," said Jaya.

"Actually, you are all right. Paper can be re-used in a lot of ways. So can iron and plastic. So, if all of you didn't pick up these things, they would be wasted and lying in places like Pallikaranai."

Velu looked around the room. So far, he had thought ragpicking was a way to earn money for food. But now he suddenly realised something else. Every child in the room did the same work that he did everyday. And there must be many more in Chennai who were not here. They all picked garbage from the bins in the city. They sorted it and sold it to dealers like Jaggu. Then the things were sold to factories. And the factories made new things with them ...

"But akka, if our work is so important, why don't we get more money for it?" Thomas asked.

Garbologists

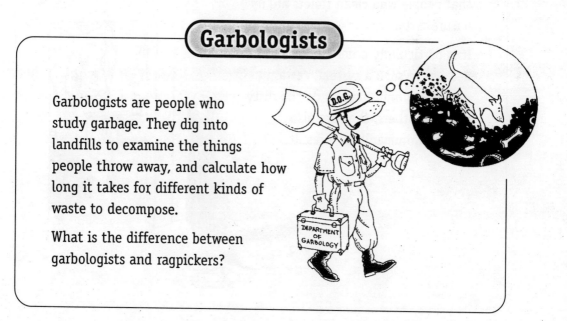

Garbologists are people who study garbage. They dig into landfills to examine the things people throw away, and calculate how long it takes for different kinds of waste to decompose.

What is the difference between garbologists and ragpickers?

Ragpickers and the Caste System

Why are ragpickers treated so badly? One important reason is the caste system in India. For many centuries, people have been divided into high and low castes. Wealthy, powerful and educated people belonged to the high castes, and prevented other castes from owning land or getting educated.

They also made rules which everyone followed: if a person is born into a certain caste, he has to do only the work of that caste. In this system, people who did manual work were considered inferior. The lowest castes were those forced to do 'dirty' work like cleaning toilets. They were considered literally 'untouchable'. Most ragpickers belong to these lowest castes.

Today, to treat someone as 'untouchable' is a crime. But the caste system has not disappeared. The high castes continue to influence all other castes. Many people still believe that those who do hard physical work are inferior, and that people who clean toilets are by nature dirty.

It is particularly cruel and unjust that because of such a system, certain people not only have to do the dirty work for others, they are also treated inhumanly as a result.

"Ha! Ask that!" Jaya said.

Bina akka didn't reply immediately. She looked at Brother.

"That's a good question, Thomas. The work is very important. But nobody looks at it that way. They think it is dirty work," Brother said.

"Yes, Brother. People chase us away when we go near them."

"And that Jaggu always pays us ten rupees less," Jaya shouted.

Viji akka looked at her. "That's how they make money. The people who buy from Jaggu pay him less so that they make more money."

Velu was still thinking about what Brother had said. He was confused. Brother said his work was important, but other people thought it was dirty. Then he realised what was bothering him.

"But it is dirty work, Brother." said Velu. "There is always a terrible smell and glass pieces cut us. I don't like it."

"Better than washing other people's dirty vessels!" Jaya butted in.

Brother looked thoughtful. "No, you're right Velu. The way it is now, it's a bad job for anybody. Viji akka's group is trying to do something about making this job a little easier. Isn't that right Viji?"

"We are going around to houses, telling people not to throw all their garbage out together. We ask them to keep vegetable peels and food waste separate from paper and plastic. And we tell them not to throw things like broken glass and syringes."

Bina akka added, "It's a little like the way you sort the garbage to make it easier for Jaggu."

"Even if you tell them all that, they still throw glass akka. Yesterday I put my foot on a broken bottle and got cut badly."

"Yes, garbage sorting should become a clean and proper job like being a bus conductor or a carpenter ..." Bina akka began.

What Ragpickers Think of Ragpicking

A group that supports working children in Chennai asked them to debate on ragpicking. These are the two sets of opinions the children came up with.

The first group said:

- We have a job and can live without begging or stealing

- We can work independently

- We help to recycle used things and keep the city clean

- We act with courage

But the second argued:

- We cannot be proud of our work

- We become more and more poor

- We become untouchables in society

- We cannot be clean

- We walk miles and miles every day

- We get hurt by glass, iron and stones and fall ill often

- We cannot go to school

- Those who are supposed to protect us harm us instead

"Akka! She's troubling me!" Jaya was trying to put a pencil into Ponni's ear.

"She pinched me first akka."

"Quiet now!" Brother said. "If you are getting restless, you can all go out and play on the swings for a while. We will have lunch in half an hour."

"Lunch! When will you give us tea?" Ponni shouted.

"I'm first for the swing!" Thomas was running for the door.

"Velu! Get up da. Sitting there like a dunce!" Jaya pulled Velu to his feet.

"Don't run away outside the compound. We have a drawing class in the afternoon," Brother said as the children ran out.

The rest of the day passed quickly. On the way back home in the evening, Velu and Jaya managed to get good seats in the bus. They sat next to each other, looking out of the window as the bus turned left into Anna Salai.

"Which dish did you like best at lunch da?"

Velu leaned back. "Which? All of them."

"Mine was the *laddu*. Look here!" From the big pocket of her pant Jaya pulled out a crushed laddu.

Velu laughed and rubbed his hands. "Super! Idea! I'll do the same tomorrow."

"Here, take half."

They sat back in their seats, munching and looking out of the window.

It was only when the bus stopped at Bells Road and everyone started to get out that Velu thought of Dorai again. The day had been full of so many new things that he had almost forgotten the hundred rupees he owed.

Suddenly the happiness flowed out of Velu. He felt like a weight had come down on him.

chapter nine

Imagine

Velu's mind was still on Dorai as they waited at the bus stop on Bells Road the next morning. He stayed close to Brother, expecting Raja and Selva to jump out and grab him any minute. But 13B arrived quickly and he jumped in before anyone else could.

Velu was nervous even when they got off the bus in Pondy Bazaar. Only when they sat down on the floor of Anbu Illam did he relax.

"See da! So much paper today. I think they'll ask us to draw again." Jaya pointed at Bina akka's table.

"All of you sit in a circle! We're going to play a game now," Bina akka began. "First we'll go back to yesterday. Remember we started talking about the work that you do? Can someone tell me where we stopped?"

"We went to play on the swings akka!"

"No, we went for lunch."

"Enough joking now. Before we did all that some of you said that you didn't like the work that you do. Others felt that it was alright."

"Akka, Jaya said it was better than washing vessels," said Arasu.

"It is!" said Jaya.

"Now imagine if you didn't have to work ..."

"How can we do that akka? I'll go hungry if I don't work!" shouted Ponni.

"I know that! I want you to try and think of what you would like to do if you had the chance."

"If I had the chance I would be an auto driver!" Thomas cried.

"That's what I mean. Think of things like that. Here are papers, colour pencils and old magazines. I want you to make a picture of what you imagine."

"I don't want to draw with pencils akka. Can I just cut out pictures?"

"Yes, yes. You can stick pictures on paper, or draw, or do both. Viji akka, Brother and I will go around and see what you have done."

Velu looked through a pile and selected a film magazine. It was full of pictures of heroes, heroines and villains. He sat down on the floor and started to look at them. He didn't feel like cutting them up.

"Aiy! Mister! Start your work. See, I've already stuck two pictures." Jaya showed Velu her paper. She had cut out a picture of a big house and one of a man wearing a suit.

"This is my house and that is my father."

"Akka said we have to draw about ourselves. You're not even in the picture."

"Keep quiet. I haven't finished. I'm inside the house, seeing a film."

Velu turned back to his magazine and thought about which picture he should cut out. He finally chose one of a fat villain being tied to a tree by a hero.

"Jaya! See, that's me thrashing Dorai nicely."

"Super da! Do one for Raja and Selva also."

Velu stuck some more pictures of villains being beaten by heroes. Then he cut out all the watches and cars he could find in the magazine and stuck them as a border around his picture.

"Velu, let's see what you have done here." Bina akka stood next to him.

"I want to teach these rowdies a lesson akka. They'll learn not to trouble children."

"Why don't you also draw some other things that you want to become? What do you like to do?"

"I like to read, akka. Shall I put one picture of an office? I can be working there."

"Good idea. Something like that." Bina akka moved on to the others.

"What about you, Thomas?"

"I don't want to sit in an office all day. This is me, driving my auto. It has a two-in-one inside with a loudspeaker on the roof. I'm taking this lady to Devi theatre, full speed."

When everyone had finished, they had to come up and show their pictures to the whole group. Brother asked them to talk about what they had done.

"These are all very interesting pictures. I hope ..." Bina akka began.

"What, akka," interrupted Thomas. "These are just for fun. They're not real."

"How can I work in an office akka? I don't even go to school," Velu said.

"Sometimes we have to work at night also akka."

"I know it is hard, Seeni. All children should have the chance to study and choose what they want to do. We would like to help you do that," Bina akka said. "If you study well in pavement school, Brother can put you in a proper school later and you will have better chances."

"Tell my mother first akka. She won't let me go for all this. I have to earn and give her the money," Ponni said.

"What is the use of school, akka!" asked Thomas. "I want to be an auto driver."

"But you need to know how to read and write even to do that."

Selvi put her hand up. "Akka! Akka!"

"Yes, Selvi?"

"Can I take my drawing home akka?"

"It's yours. You can keep it."

"She has rolled up a colour pencil inside her drawing, Brother!"

"Lies, Brother!"

"Akka, I want to drink water."

"Quiet! Alright, we'll stop for today, but I want you to think about what we have said."

"Finished? No lunch today Brother?" Ponni asked.

"We will have lunch now, but after that you are free."

"Can we go and play on the swings Brother?"

Support for Street Children

Velu, Jaya and their friends enjoy the workshop. Who conducts such workshops for children like them? There are organisations in several Indian cities which support and help street and working children. Some of them conduct classes which prepare children to go to school. Others run schools themselves. Some others run shelter homes at which children like Velu can stay. Shelter homes also have recreation centres where working children can rest, play, read or learn creative skills.

Some organisations have help desks at railway stations. The people at these desks look for children like Velu, who have run away from their villages and come to the city. They take them to shelter homes. They then either help them to go back home, or support them while they learn to make a living in the city.

Many of these organisations help the children learn a trade or skill and even find jobs for them.

"Yes, of course. But quietly. The T. Nagar children will be having their class here in the afternoon. And we are starting half an hour earlier tomorrow. Because it is the last day we have arranged an outing for you."

The last day! A shock went through Velu. All afternoon his head had buzzed with different thoughts—working in an office, having money, meeting his sisters again ... but what was the use thinking about such things? Dorai was waiting for him. And he didn't even have ten rupees, let alone the hundred he was supposed to pay.

"What outing Brother? Where are you taking us?" Jaya asked.

"Come tomorrow, you'll see."

After lunch, some of the children stayed back to play. Velu wandered out into the compound.

"Aiy Velu, push me on the swing," Jaya tugged at Velu's shirt.

Velu pushed her away.

"What's wrong with you glumface? Don't want to play?"

Velu sat down on the ground and didn't answer.

"Che! Come on da."

"Dorai is waiting to kill me!" Velu burst out.

Jaya stared at him.

"Tomorrow is the last day! And I don't even have ten rupees. Dorai will really finish me. What's the use of playing and drawing all these things?"

"Oh. That's what it is."

"I'm going back to work now. At least I can get five or ten rupees," Velu stood up.

"I'll come with you."

Velu and Jaya walked past the playground. Suddenly, Velu stopped. "But if we go to Jaggu, Raja and Selva will catch me."

"Don't worry da. You stay out of the way. I'll take everything and go."

As they made their way back, Velu felt pressed down with a heavy weight. Would he ever be able to get out of this mess?

chapter ten

Out of the City

The next day was no better. Velu had slept badly, afraid all night that the morning would come. Even when he dozed off for a while, a dull voice kept repeating "Hundred rupees! Hundred rupees!" in his head. Though he had managed to avoid Dorai, Velu had only earned eight rupees the previous evening.

He let Jaya drag him to Bells Road and followed Brother into the bus. They all got off a while later, and boarded another bus at Saidapet. Velu sat by a window and watched the city passing by him for almost two hours.

Only when it drove out of the city, past checkposts and open fields did he realise that they were going somewhere else that day. He looked around for Jaya but she was sitting with Ponni, two seats ahead of him. The man next to Velu was asleep, snoring. Velu yawned and closed his eyes.

"Dai! Hurry up, we have to get down!" Thomas shook Velu awake.

Velu squeezed out of the bus and stepped onto the road. His eyes flew from side to side automatically, looking for Dorai. But there was no one around except an old man selling coconuts. He could see no buildings or shops on the side of the road, only a few palm trees. On the other side was a huge compound wall with a blue gate. Where were they?

"What is this surprise outing Brother? Why have we got off here? There is nothing to see," Jaya said.

"This building is a paper factory. We have brought you here so that you can see for yourself how paper is made," Brother pointed.

"Now you can get an idea of what happens to all the paper you pick up from the bins," Viji akka said.

"Do they make coloured paper here?" asked Ponni.

"Will they let us take some paper home?" Jaya wanted to know.

"We will find out inside. You can ask all your questions there. Everyone follow me now. Go through the gate one by one," Brother said.

They crossed over to the other side of the road. *KJS Paper Works*, Velu read the sign that was painted on the gate. He yawned and walked slowly behind Bina akka. Jaya and Thomas pushed past him and ran into the compound.

"Aiy, look! Let's swing on those pipes!" Jaya shouted.

"We can jump on the hay!" said Thomas.

"Oy Velu, come on da! Where are you looking? Try to find me," said Jaya and disappeared behind a huge stack of hay.

Velu still felt dazed. He looked around vaguely at the big buildings and the things piled up against the walls.

"Aiy! Boy! Side, side." A man in a small truck swerved around Velu.

"Jaya! Thomas! Don't touch anything in this place. Come here now. There are electric lines there," Brother shouted.

The children waited with Brother while Bina and Viji akka went into the building. They came out with a short man in a blue uniform. He walked over and shook Brother's hand.

"This is Mr. Paramesvaran," explained Viji akka. "He will show us all around the factory. You can ask him any questions you like."

"Welcome to all of you. Before we go into the factory, I want to tell you that this is the first time that we are letting children inside this area. It is only because we know Ms. Viji that we agreed. You must not run around or touch anything. We have pipes of boiling water, acid and electricity lines here and you can get hurt if you go near them. Please follow me one by one and hold each other by the hand."

Everyone fell silent and quietly followed the man into the building. He led them into a big room and up a narrow metal staircase that creaked and swayed with every step. The room was filled with clanking and hissing noises. Steam rose up from the ground below them as they climbed.

"Put your feet carefully here. Don't slip. This is where we boil and pulp the raw material for paper. Some factories use wood, but we use sugarcane fibres," shouted Mr. Paramesvaran as they went up the stairs.

Below them Velu saw a row of huge metal pots full of boiling pulp. He dragged his feet behind Jaya. As they reached the top, Velu's foot caught on a stair and he stumbled. Jaya pulled him up.

"Careful! One wrong step and pachak!" said Jaya, grimacing. "What da? You look like a ghost has caught hold of you today."

"Quiet. No fooling around," said Viji akka from behind them.

They walked along a balcony above the room, looking down. A group of men were shovelling what looked like bits of paper into the boiling pots.

"Anna, what are they throwing in?" Arasu asked Mr. Paramesvaran.

"It's paper da! I can see from here," Thomas shouted.

"Are they making new paper from it?" Ponni asked.

"Yes, that is old white paper. You probably pick up paper like this. It is good raw material for us to add to the pulp. We shred it into small pieces. Then we put it in chemicals to make it colourless and clean."

"You mean what we sell to Jaggu comes over here and becomes new paper?" Jaya asked.

"That is what Mr. Paramesvaran is saying. The paper that you pick up is boiled in those pots and used again," Brother explained.

"See da! That man is boiling some paper that I picked last week." Thomas nudged Arasu.

"So how much does that Jaggu get for selling it here?" Jaya looked at Brother. "I'm sure he cheats them also."

"Ayyo! My hand!" Arasu cried suddenly.

"What happened?" Mr. Paramesvaran ran to him.

"That pipe burned me!"

"Careful! There is steam in those pipes. I told you not to touch anything!"

Mr. Paramesvaran poured some cold water on Arasu's hand. Then he led them on to another room. There was a row of big machines into which people were pouring pulp.

"After the pulp boils and becomes thick, we put it into this machine. It presses and squeezes out the water from the pulp. Then it goes into a roller which flattens it out."

"Look da! How it comes!" said Seeni.

Tree-free paper

Some paper mills make recycled paper out of used paper and rags. Others use jute, bamboo, and sugarcane or rice straw as raw materials. Paper which does not use wood pulp as raw material is known as 'tree-free' paper.

Tree-free paper can be of two kinds—either made by machine, or by hand. Machine-made paper is cheaper, but the factories which produce such paper are large, using a lot of electricity, water and chemicals. A hand-made paper unit is usually small, uses far less electricity and water, and produces less waste. Hand-made paper is more expensive, but has interesting colours, textures and forms.

Paper made from rags, bagasse (sugar cane wastes) straw, cereal stalks, used paper etc. is called 'tree-free' or 'recycled' or 'eco-friendly' paper.

Velu watched as the pulp was poured in and came out as wet, thin sheets.

"Each of these papers is as long as a bus!" Jaya said.

Mr. Paramesvaran took them to the next room. It was hot and steamy and the wet sheets from the roller were being passed over big drums.

The First Paper

T'sai Lun, an official in the court of the Chinese Emperor in 105 A.D., is said to have made the first paper. He beat up old fishing nets, rags and ropes in running water, and spread the pulp on a screen of fine bamboo strips and dried it in the sun.

Paper reached India around the 12th century.

"This is the drying room. Those drums are heated from inside. The sheets become dry after they are rolled over the drums. Then they are pressed again to flatten them out and kept ready for cutting. Here, this way."

Make Your Own Paper

You will need:

- cardboard (several pieces)
- an old bucket
- 4 table spoons of maida flour
- food grinder
- old newspaper (about 10 double sheets)

- a sieve
- hot water
- pieces of old cloth
- a few bricks

1. Tear up the newspaper. Soak it in hot water overnight and drain.

2. Make a paste with flour and water and add it to the paper.

3. Grind this in a food grinder until you get a thick paste.

4. Put a bit of the paste on the sieve and press out excess water to form a sheet-like layer of paper. Invert this onto a piece of cloth.

5. Cover with another piece of cloth, and add another layer of wet paper. Repeat until you have a stack of 4-5 sheets of paper.

6. Place a piece of cardboard on the stack and weigh it down with bricks. Leave the stack out to dry.

7. When it has dried, you can peel off the layers of paper.

The Story of a Paper Mill in Karnataka

A paper mill was set up near a bamboo forest owned by the government. The mill used bamboo as raw material.

As the demand for paper grew, the factory began to produce more, needing more bamboo. Soon there was not enough bamboo left in the forest. They had to bring in raw materials from the surrounding areas.

Soon the production was so huge that even this was not enough. The mill began to look for other forests, farther away. It looks like we will soon run out of forests.

As they left the room, Mr. Paramesvaran tore off a bit of paper from a huge roll and passed it around.

"Here, touch. See how smooth it is."

Velu touched the new paper carefully. It smelt fresh and clean.

"This came out of a garbage bin?" He passed it to Jaya.

In the last room, rolls and rolls of fresh paper were stacked against the wall. Some men cut up the rolls into sheets, using huge machines. A group of women moved around the room, stacking the cut sheets neatly into bundles. On their way out, Mr. Paramesvaran gave each of the children a few sheets each.

"You can use them in your school," he said.

"Let's all thank Mr. Paramesvaran, he has to go back to work now," Brother began. "Now you have an idea of how your work is imp ..."

Work! thought Velu. Jam Bazaar! I have to go back to all that tomorrow. He felt the fear coming back. He looked up to see Mr. Paramesvaran pointing at something and speaking, but he didn't hear what he said.

"They're giving us food in their canteen. Come on da!" Jaya tugged at Velu's shirt. Velu followed her.

"What are you gong to do with your paper? I'm not going to write and all. See this, I've made a motor boat." Thomas ran up, waving something at them. He pushed a paper boat in Velu's face.

"I'm going to go full speed down Buckingham Canal," he said. "Right through the whole of Chennai."

"Hopes! You'll get stuck in the muck in Triplicane itself," sneered Jaya.

At the canteen, everyone got a big tray of food for themselves.

Buckingham Canal

The Buckingham Canal in
Chennai was planned as a
waterway for boats and small
ships, meant to carry people
and goods all the way to
Southern Orissa. At the
beginning of the twentieth
century, you could sail all the
way down the canal, through
Chennai. Sadly, it is now just a foul
sewer, choked with garbage.

"Look at this! They've given us laddus! Dai Velu! Remember that laddu we got from the workshop? Let's take one from here also," Jaya was nudging him excitedly.

"Ah?" Velu was picking at his chapati. "Laddu?"

"You're really a blockhead! Since morning you've been like this." Jaya ate up her laddu and walked away.

No use telling her, thought Velu, watching her go. She'll just say hide for two more days, make some money.

He ate slowly, not even tasting his food. When the bus stops at Saidapet, should I slip out of the door? I can take a train and go somewhere. But where? Maybe I'll have to stay on the train, cleaning the floor.

Velu sat at the table alone, his head spinning. There was no way out. It was hopeless, this would be his last day. He closed his eyes and put his head down on the table. In the background he heard Bina akka calling everyone. He didn't bother to lift his head up and see what it was about.

"Please come out and sit on the steps. We will not be going back to Anbu Illam from here, so I want to give this to you before we all …"

Her voice faded away and Velu drifted off.

"Velu! Velu! Get up da! You've slept off right here! I was looking for you."

Velu opened his eyes and blinked. He was still there.

"Akka is calling you! Don't sit like a lump. Take your envelope!"

Velu stared at Jaya.

"Envelope?"

"Hundred rupees da! Hundred rupees!" shouted Jaya, waving a brown envelope.

Hundred rupees? He was surely dreaming.

"Oh there you are." Bina akka walked over to Velu. "You're the only one left." She handed him an envelope like Jaya's.

Velu took it. It felt real, this couldn't be a dream!

"What's this akka?"

"Keep it, it's for you. We usually do this when we have workshops. Since you came to the workshop for three days, you couldn't earn anything. That's why we're giving it to everyone who came."

Velu tore open the envelope. There were two fifty rupee notes inside. Hundred rupees! He was saved! ·

"Say thanks da!" Jaya whispered into his ear.

"Thanks akka. Thanks!" Velu said loudly.

"Ayyo! Why are you shouting suddenly! Till now you were lying here like a dead snake." Jaya looked at him curiously.

"Hundred rupees Jaya!" Velu clutched the notes.

"So, ten movies this week?" she asked slyly. "Or what?"

"No chance! I'm going to give Dorai his money back. I don't want to see this hundred rupees again."

"Why give it all to that loafer? Give him half now and the rest slowly."

"Nothing. Let that headache be finished. I'm giving it to him this evening."

"Your money, your wish," said Jaya.

In the bus on the way back, Velu could hardly stay still. He kept counting the two notes to check that they were actually there. What a piece of luck. He felt like jumping out of the bus with happiness.

Velu looked out of the window. They must have passed all this in the morning but he hadn't seen anything. Women carried bundles of paddy through the fields. A small boy sat near the road, watching over his cows. Maybe they've started cutting the paddy at home, he thought.

He turned around to show Jaya the fields, but she had slept off. Brother was sitting next to her, reading a paper. Before he knew it, the fields disappeared and they entered the city.

Child Workers Speak for Themselves

In November 1996, twenty-nine child workers from Asia, Africa and South America met in Bangalore, to discuss their lives, work and plans for the future. They came up with this list of demands:

- We want people to respect the work we do

- We want an education suitable to our needs and skills.

- We want access to good health care.

- We want to be consulted on all decisions concerning us.

- We want living and working conditions in villages to be improved, so that we do not have to migrate to cities.

- We do not want to be ill-treated at work. We are for work but we also want time for education, play and rest.

- We want poverty, the main cause of our problem, to be removed.

Like Jaya, Velu, and Dasan and other children in this book, the children who made these important demands think clearly and intelligently. They ask for better living and working conditions and time to learn and play.

Yet when we think about it, these children still take one thing for granted—that they will continue to work for a living. In their situation, it is difficult for them to think of a world in which they do not have to work in order to survive.

No child should have to work to earn a living. Every child should be able to learn, play and be carefree.

In Real Life

Velu's story has probably left you with a lot of questions. Have things gone well for him? Through a stroke of luck, he gets the money he owes Dorai, and his immediate problem is solved. But what about in the longer run? Will he have to continue ragpicking though he dislikes it?

From the way the story ends, it seems that things have not really changed for children like Velu and Jaya. They still have to continue to work. When we wrote the story, we wanted to have a happy end, in which Velu and Jaya do not need to work anymore. But then we decided to keep our story as close as possible to the real lives of working children, as they are today.

As we have pointed out in this book, there are many reasons why children are still forced to work for a living. Although there are concerned people and groups working for their welfare, their lives can't change all of a sudden. But does this mean we can't do anything?

Not at all. Of course these problems can't be solved simply. But it is important not to ignore them, and to face up to the fact that they exist. We hope that reading this book has helped you know and understand a little more about working children. All of you must have seen such children—ragpicking, working in restaurants, in garages, or as servants in houses. You may have felt troubled and had questions about their lives. Such questions are important, so we have tried to deal with some of them. After reading this book, you may want to share your thoughts and feelings with your friends, parents or teachers.

The second thing we have looked at in the book is the actual work ragpickers do. It is connected to waste recycling and the environment. Some of these issues are again very large. You may feel that you cannot do much as an individual, for instance, if factories dump all their waste into rivers.

Yet groups of people who are concerned about the environment have got together and changed things. Even as an individual, it is not too difficult to contribute towards keeping your environment clean. Basically, you need to be always aware of how each thing you do or use affects the environment.

Finally, here are a few practical suggestions for those of you who decide to actively do something about some of the issues raised in this book.

Child Labour

1. Get in touch with an organisation in your city that supports child workers, and see if they need any help.

2. You could donate books, clothes or schoolbags to such organisations for the children they support.

3. You could offer to teach the children to read and write or even teach some of the more advanced students a subject that you are good at.

4. Many groups organise protests and action against specific issues. For example, they visit schools just before Diwali to tell children that they must not buy firecrackers made in factories that employ child labour. You could help with such campaigns in your neighbourhood or at your school.

5. Subscribe to newsletters of such organisations so that you know what is being done, and how you can contribute.

6. Talk to friends, have discussions in school and at home, so that more people become aware of the problem and understand it.

Garbage Disposal and the Environment

1. The book suggests many ways in which you can help reduce waste that is harmful to the environment. Try to implement these in your home and at school.

2. Contact environmental activists in your city, and find out what you can do to help them. You could invite some of these activists to your school to talk about their work.

3. Many of these groups organise activities to clean up parts of the city. You could participate in such activities and encourage your friends to join as well.

4. There are many books available that tell you about environment and ecology. Try and find these books in your school or your local library and have discussions with your teachers and classmates about them. Subscribe to newsletters of organisations working for the environment so that you know what is being done, and how you can contribute.

5. You need to be continually aware of how each thing you do or use affects the environment. If you don't know, find out by reading or asking people. You can also come up with your own ideas on how to reduce or recycle the things you use.

6. Most importantly, you must talk about these things with your friends and your family. If every individual does his or her bit towards reducing waste, it will make a big difference to the total amount of garbage that goes out into the environment.

Acknowledgments

We are grateful to Friar. Jesu, ofm and the children of Nesakkaram, Street Elfins Education and Development Society (SEEDS), for making this book possible.

We would like to thank the Tatachem Golden Jubilee Foundation for sponsoring the workshop with street children, the members of Mylapore Children's Club, Chennai who participated, and Dr. Neeraja Raghavan for helping with the workshops.

The Handmade Paper Industry, Aurobindo Ashram and the paper factory at Mailam Industrial Estate, Pondicherry, made it possible for the children to visit their units and learn about the process of papermaking.

Anita Moorthy helped with the preliminary research for the book. Vikram R. Vasu and S. Sathya of The School-KFI, Chennai contributed useful material about recycling.

C.K. Meena's article "Adults Before Their Time" which appeared in *The Hindu*, Feb 2, 1997 and "Does Ragpicking Promote or Destroy Human Dignity?" from *Journey with Street Children*—SEEDS, 1988-98 were extremely useful in helping us present child workers' views of their own lives.

Heinz and Anita Leutwiler, Mohan Sampath, EMW Hamburg, Judith Uyterlinde, Agna Rudolph, Maryan Klomp, N. S. Raja and Ekko Smith contributed generously in subsidising this book for the reader.

Praise for Trash!

"Without causing guilt in the young reader, *Trash!* succeeds in bringing about empathy and is a catalyst for constructive action."

The Hindu, July 30, 1999

"*Trash!* is a big step towards awakening a sense of responsibility in the younger generation ... to a basic civic issue."

The Economic Times, Madras Plus, August 5, 1999

"The anonymous ragpicker is on every street picking discarded footwear and clothes. *Trash!* lifts the ragpicker out of his anonymity and places him centre-stage."

Deccan Chronicle, December 12, 1999

"Based on well-researched material, and an absorbing story-line, *Trash!* guides a young reader into the world of waste collectors. ... The quality and content of the book is further enriched by the witty and imaginative illustrations of Orijit Sen."

The Hindu, Literary Review, March 5, 2000

"The book is so pleasantly and artistically produced but with such a heart-rending story, that it sails like a dream."

The Deccan Herald, April 8, 2000

TARA PUBLISHING

Books with Perspective

Based in the Indian context, Tara books are original, enjoyable and contemporary. They range from novels, picture books and nonsense verse, to translations from Indian languages, gender and environment themes

For ages 4 and above

- Alphabets are Amazing Animals
- Babu the Waiter
- Ponni the Flower Seller
- Catch That Crocodile
- Monkey's Drum
- Tiger on a Tree
- The Fivetongued Firefanged Folkadotted Dragon Snake
- The Very Hungry Lion
- HenSparrow Turns Purple

For ages 8 and above

- A Wild Elephant at Camp
- African Tales from Tendai's Grandmother
- Anything but a Grabooberry
- The Spectacular Spectacle Man
- Toys and Tales with Everyday Materials
- Excuse Me, IsThis India?
- Wish You Were Here

For ages 10 and above

- Child Art with Everyday Materials
- Four Heroes and a Haunted House
- Four Heroes and a Green Beard
- Landscapes: Children's Voices

- Leaf Life
- Puppets Unlimited with Everyday Materials
- The Mahabharatha
- Toys and Tales with Everyday Materials
- Trash! On Ragpicker Children and Recycling

For young adults

- Real Men Don't Pick Peonies (On an Alpine-style Ascent)

For adults/parents and educators

- Child Art with Everyday Materials
- Landscapes: Children's Voices
- Leaf Life
- Picturing Words & Reading Pictures
- Puppets Unlimited with Everyday Materials
- Toys and Tales with Everyday Materials
- Trash! On Ragpicker Children and Recycling
- Masks and Performance with Everyday Materials